ENGLISH PLAYBOOK

JN102678

同志社女子大学英語英文学会（編）

EIHŌSHA

語彙学習を楽しむ旅へ

この本に興味を持って頂きありがとうございます。

みなさんは Vocabulary，語彙学習と聞くと何が頭に浮かぶでしょうか？小テスト，一夜漬け，大学受験⁉ では当時の語彙のおぼえ方は？ひたすら，書く・読む・見る⁉ この 3 つまたはその組み合わせなのではないでしょうか。いずれにしても辛い思い出なのかもしれません。

その反動からか，IELTS/TOEFL/TOEIC などの試験対策をのぞけば，大学に入ってからも（卒業してからも）高校時代と同じように語彙学習を続けている人は少ないのが実情です。高校卒業時に「大学に入ってからも高校時代と同じ気持ちで勉強すれば必ずや成功する」と言われた記憶のある人もいると思いますが，実際には大学に入るとなかなかその通り実行することは難しいようです。

それは学習者の問題かもしれませんが，周りをよく見渡してみると語彙集にも問題があるようです。現在出版されている語彙集，ベストセラーと評判のものですら，よほどのモチベーションがない限り続かない仕組みになっているのです。「これこそ本命！」と次々に新たな語彙集を出版するための conspiracy（陰謀）ではないかしらと疑いたくなるくらいです。

一方で学習者の側にも問題があります。授業に参加するだけで英語能力が上がると思っている学生諸姉が数多くいます。授業参加は当然ですが，それだけでは十分ではありません。おぼえる努力なしに「自然に語彙習得」するにはその語彙に「16 回」（平均）出会う必要があるというのが定説です（Lightbown & Spada, 2021 による）。例えば 応用言語学（Applied Linguistics）のゼミ学生諸姉は全員，acquisition（習得）と いうやや高度な語彙を知っています。これは毎回ゼミでこの単語が出てくるため自然と覚えてしまうのです。残念ながらこのような自然習得する語彙は数が限られています。

つまり，語彙学習においては適切な題材を参考に意図的に工夫しながら学び続ける必要があるのです。この語彙集はそのような企図のもと，みなさんのために

制作されたものです。本書は 2017 年に同志社女子大学英語英文学会設立 50 周年記念として企画・制作された旧版『English Playbook』をさらに読みやすく使いやすくなるよう，再度編集委員が目を通し，加筆・修正しました。以下，3 つの特徴を御紹介します。

① 楽しく・戦略的に学ぶ：

語彙学習を効果的にするためには「楽しく学ぶ」ことを忘れるわけにはいきません。

本書のタイトルになっている（English）"Playbook" とは文字通り「楽しむ本」ということです。Play にはもともと「遊ぶ」という意味があります。言葉は楽しいし，学ぶことは楽しい。学んだことを実践し，それを積み重ねていくことは，自分へのご褒美となります。また，"Playbook" とはサッカーやアメリカンフットボールでのゲーム戦略や戦術をまとめた本のことでもあります。本書は，アスリートのようにストラテジー（戦略）を練って，読者の皆さんが，自分を鍛え，さまざまなコミュニケーションの場面に対応できるように構成されています（詳細は本書の使い方の項参照）。

② 現実的使用観点からの語彙選択：

大学での学びや英語使用時の必要性，日本人大学生に誤用の多いものという観点から語彙を選択しました。 難解な語彙すなわち高級な語彙とは考えていません。高校までに学習済みの語彙も含まれていますが，そのような語彙はこのようなことを知っておかないと実際には使うことができませんよ，という要注意語彙でもあります。特に既に知っている語彙については Note のコメントをよく読んでください。

③ 教員の普段の授業・研究の知見の蓄積を基礎に語彙選択：

使用頻度順に配列したコーパスベースの通常の語彙集とは異なり，大学の英語関連の各分野（文学・文化・言語・コミュニケーション）で教える教員が授業・研究・日々のコミュニケーションに必要な語彙として推薦した 400 語に厳選しました。従って，出現頻度は低いがある分野では必須の語彙であるものが含まれています。

Playbook には実はもうひとつの意味があります。それは演劇のリハーサルで使われるような「芝居の台本が入った本」のことです。シェイクスピアが "All the world's a stage, and all the men and women merely players."（この世はすべて舞台，ひとは人生の役を演じているだけ）と喝破したように，本書は，読者のみなさんが自分の配役をうまく演じられるように作られたともいえます。英語の学びはひとつひとつ目標を達成しながらも生涯学ぶことのできるものです。英語学習に臨界期はありません。特に語彙学習は人生最後の日まで続けることができるものです。自分の人生の台本としても活用して頂きたいと念願しています。特に，本書を手にして頂いた大学卒業生の皆様にとっても，この Playbook が英語学習そしてその先にある素晴らしい世界への扉となりますことを祈念しています。

　最後になりましたが，この語彙集作成にあたり，多くの皆様にご協力を賜りました。2016 年度在籍の同志社女子大学表象文化学部・英語英文学科の先生方には本文の執筆を，在学生のみなさんには語彙選択についての貴重なアイデアを提供して頂きました。6 名の学生諸姉には本書最大の特長ともいえるイラストを大学生の視点から描いて頂きました。また狩野裕也様には 2018 年度版の構成を一緒に考えて頂き，英語英文学会事務局には出版に関わる諸業務を一手に引き受けて頂きました。そして英宝社（株）下村幸一様には本書の出版の労を執って頂きました。厚く感謝申し上げます。

「旅の終わりは旅のはじまり」
（映画『旅芸人の記録』テオ・アンゲロプロス，1975 年より）

English Playbook 編集委員会

目　　次

テキストの音声は、
弊社 HP　https://www.eihosha.co.jp/text/
978-4-269-63011-6.html
の「テキスト音声ダウンロード」のバナーから
ダウンロードできます。また、右記 QR コードを
読み込み、音声ファイルをダウンロードするか、
ストリーミングページにジャンプして音声を聴くことができます。

音声データ

本書の説明

　この Playbook には，英語学習・研究に役立つ 400 項目が 4 エリアに分けて掲載されています。それぞれ 100 語毎に区切り，Part Ⅰ：Exploration（探索）→ Part Ⅱ：Discovery（発見）→ Part Ⅲ：Transition（転換）→ Part Ⅳ：Accomplishment（達成）と順を追って語彙が難しくなるよう配列されていますが，各自の興味に合わせてどこからでも学習を開始することができます。

エリア 1 ─────────────── エリア 3

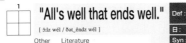

1 "All's well that ends well."

[ɔ́ːdz wél / ðæt_éndz wél]

Other　Literature

Def : used to indicate that the situation turned out well after all

日 : 終わりよければすべてよし（シェイクスピア）

Syn : happy ending

e.g. : "We got lost on the way but finally made it on time. **All's well that ends well.**"（途中で道に迷ったが、どうにか間に合いました。やれやれ）

Notes : This title of Shakespeare's play is often used to indicate relief at a happy ending. 英語の諺みたいになっていますから、そのまま覚えて使いましょう。ひやひやしたが結局大丈夫だった、とほっとしたときに使う言葉です。

エリア 2 ─────────────── エリア 4

エリア 1
　ターゲットワード、発音、品詞、よく使われる分野表示。自己チェック用に 4 分割空欄を用意、○や△、塗りつぶしなど自分でマークを決めて利用してください。
＜分野表示＞
　基礎（Basic）基盤的語彙　　　学術（Academic）学術研究全般
＜特定学術分野＞
　文学（Literature）　　　文化（Culture）　　　言語学（Linguistics）
　コミュニケーション（Communication）　　　会話（Conversation）日常会話
　時事（Current）新聞ニュース
　テスト（TOEIC）TOEIC テストでよく出題されるもの
エリア 2
　関連するイラストと例文を掲載。但し、イラストは必ずしも例文を説明するものではありません。
エリア 3
　英語定義と訳語、似たような意味を持つ単語やフレーズ（類義語）を表示。「NA」（該当なし）はその項目の類義語がないことを示しています。
エリア 4
　ターゲットワードの活用方法、誤用例などその他有用情報を記載。

活用方法（基礎編）

A. 絵の利用・エピソードの利用・発音の活用

　　ターゲットワードとセットになっているイラストを活用しましょう。イメージと英単語を結びつけるのは効果的な記憶方略です。覚えにくい単語は自分自身でもイラストを描いてみましょう。また，各語彙には読みもの（エピソード，アドバイス，失敗談など）が用意されています。「お話」は記憶に残りやすいものです（エピソード記憶）。じっくりと読み単語と結びつけて下さい。同時に発音を聞くことが出来るよう QR コードが掲載されています。モデルの音声を聞きながら発音記号をみて，自分で 5 回発音してみましょう。

B. セルフテスト（Self Test）

　　カードを用意してエリア 1〜4 のいずれかを隠して，その中の情報を覚えるようにします。例えば，エリア 1 と 3 を隠しエリア 2 と 4 の情報だけを見て，単語，発音，絵，例文を覚えるようにします。定期的に自分の理解を試してみましょう。

C. 自己調整学習

　　自分でゴールを決めましょう。たとえば，1 週間で 20 語覚えるとすれば次の A と B ではどちらの方がより効果があるでしょうか？

　　（A）毎日 3 語ずつ確実におぼえる

　　（B）毎日 20 語目を通し，おぼえていない単語に集中する

　　正解は（B）。これは認知心理学の成果が示すところです。1 ヶ月で 100 語おぼえる際にも同様に毎日 100 語目を通し，弱点の単語に集中するのです。その際，自己チェック用の 4 つの空欄（エリア 1）は有効だと思います。

活用方法（上級編）

D. 検索する：

　　本，雑誌，新聞，そしてコースのリーディングで，多くの単語を見つけることができます。Playbook に載っている単語を英語リーディングの中で見つけると，実際にその「意味」を見ることができ，その背景にある意味や感情，歴史を理解することができます。

E. 聞く：

　　ポッドキャストでも，TEDトークでも，英語の授業のリスニング練習でも，あるいは先生が話しているのを聞くのでも，英語を聞いているときにPlaybookに載っている単語を聞き取れるようにしましょう。実際の英会話を自分の耳で聞くことで，これらの単語との出会いを楽しむことができます！

F. 使う：

　　最もやりがいがあり，効果的な方法は，Playbookに載っている単語を実際に自分の英語で使ってみることです！先生やクラスメートと話したり，文章を書いたり，プレゼンテーションをしたりするときに，Playbookに載っているいろいろな単語を使ってみてください。Playbookにある語彙を使えば使うほど，満足感と自己効力感が高まります。

G. 新しい語彙リスト

　　新しい語彙を体系的に復習することに慣れてきたら，新しい語彙のリストを自分で作り，徹底的に調べて，このPlaybookと同じような形式で自分だけの語彙集を作ることをお勧めします。できあがったら友人と共有してみましょう。

学習のリフレッシュに

　　ストラテジーとならんで重要なのが学習意欲（動機）の維持です。各ページ（下）には教員が選び抜いた珠玉の名言100を紹介しています。英語学習に人生にすこし疲れたらこれらの言葉から何かの力を得てください。

付録：日本人英語学習者がよく間違える英語30

　　英語を使うとミスは必ずおきます。これは必然的なものです。しかし，それらのミスは理由が分かればすぐに修正できるものです。教員が日頃教えている中で気づいた日本人英語学習者によく見られるミスを30個厳選しました。英語を使う前，使った後に参照してください。

Part 1

Exploration

Again, you can't connect the dots looking forward;
you can only connect them looking backwards.
So you have to trust that the dots will somehow connect in your future.

You have to trust in something — your gut, destiny, life, karma, whatever.
This approach has never let me down, and it has made all the difference in my life.

(Steve Jobs, 2005)

Jobs, S. (June 12, 2005). *'You've got to find what you love,' Jobs says*. Stanford University News. https://news.stanford.edu/2005/06/12/youve-got-find-love-jobs-says/

1

"All's well that ends well."

[ɔ́:lz wél / ðət_éndz wél]

Other　Literature

Def : used to indicate that the situation turned out well after all

日 : 終わりよければすべてよし（シェイクスピア）

Syn : happy ending

e.g. : "We got lost on the way but finally made it on time. **All's well that ends well.**" （途中で道に迷ったが、どうにか間に合いました。やれやれ）

Notes : This title of Shakespeare's play is often used to indicate relief at a happy ending. 英語の諺みたいになっていますから、そのまま覚えて使いましょう。ひやひやしたが結局大丈夫だった、とほっとしたときに使う言葉です。

2

claim

[kléɪm]

Verb　Basic

Def : say that something is true, without offering proof

日 : 〜と主張する

Syn : assert

e.g. : My neighbor **claims** that he saw a UFO. （隣の人は UFO を見た、と主張しています）

Notes : 日本語のクレームが意味する「文句を言う」という意味合いはないので気をつけましょう。argue と同様に主張するという意味でよく使われますが、例文にあるように、証拠がなく、その主張の信憑性に疑問が残る点が argue と違う点です。

3

summarize

[sʌ́məràɪz]

Verb　Academic

Def : express the meaning of a text in a shorter form

日 : 要約する

Syn : sum up

e.g. : The teacher asked the students to **summarize** their main points in their essay's conclusion. （先生は結論でエッセイの要点をまとめるようにと言った）

Notes : Summarizing means giving a short version of something, including the main points, but omitting details and examples. 要約するとは、重要な点は含みながらも細部や例を除外して短縮版を作成することです。英語を聞いたり、読んだりした際には特に要約は重要となります。名詞形は summary（要約）ですが、summery は「夏らしい」という意味なので、スペルに要注意！

4

lecture

[léktʃər]

Noun　Academic

Def : a long, serious speech given as a scolding

日 : 説教

Syn : a talking-to

e.g. : He got a **lecture** about the importance of recycling. （リサイクルの大切さについて、延々と説教をくらった）

Notes : I learned a lot about Japan by watching *Sazae-san*, and I was interested by the formal way Namihei lectures poor Katsuo. サザエさんは日本語や日本文化の学習にいいようですね。

（一口アドバイス）1　Noticing is learning. Keep your eyes and ears open!

5 be into

[bɪ ɪ́ntu:]

Verb　Current

Def: be strongly interested in (informal)

日: ～に夢中

Syn: be crazy about

e.g.: I'm really **into** rock music. (私は本当にロックミュージックが好きだ)

Notes: A slang word commonly used when talking about sports, music, food, etc.--things that you particularly love. 日本語に訳すと into は～に「入り込む」という意味ですが、「夢中になること」と同じですね。会話で使ってみましょう。

---

6 "It's up to you."

[ɪts_ʌ́(p)_tu jú:]

Other　Conversation

Def: It's your choice.

日: あなた次第です

Syn: whichever/whatever you like

e.g.: "Do you want Italian or French?" **"It's up to you."** (イタリア料理にしようか、それともフランス料理がいい？　君次第さ)

Notes: 日本人は遠慮がちと言われますが、もじもじしていると「早くして」とこのセリフが飛んできます。「でも～」とさらにもじもじしたりしないでバシッと決めないと、海外生活ではメンドくさいやつだと思われるので注意しましょう。

---

7 range

[réɪndʒ]

Verb　Academic

Def: change within limits

日: ～に及ぶ、変動する

Syn: stretch, vary

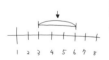

e.g.: Its prices **range** from ¥5,000 to ¥50,000. (その値段は、5,000 円から50,000 円まで様々です)

Notes: "range from A to B" (A から B まで様々な) の形でよく見かける単語です。名詞形でもよく使われます。"temperature range" というと「温度の変動域」という意味になります。

---

8 diagnosis

[dàɪəgnóusɪs]

Noun　Academic

Def: a doctor's opinion of what is wrong with a sick person

日: 診断

Syn: NA

e.g.: After making the **diagnosis**, the doctor prescribed medicine. (医者は診断をして薬を処方した)

Notes: Contrast this with "prognosis": A diagnosis is the labeling of a medical condition. A prognosis is the predicted outcome of the condition. "prognosis" は「治療をした後の予測」となりますので相違に気をつけましょう。

（一口アドバイス）2　Go the distance. (Hercules)

9 "How do you spell that?"

[hâu du ju spél ðæt]

Other　Conversation

Def : used to ask the spelling of a word

日 : どう綴りますか？ スペルは？

Syn : What's the spelling?"

e.g. : "Professor Oda, **how do you spell** 'acquisition'?"（小田先生、習得という意味の acquisition はどのような綴りですか）

Notes : This expression is basic and useful, but many students still don't use it. よく使う質問ですが英語で表現するとなるとなかなか出てこないのも事実ですね。授業で使ってみましょう。

---

10 get it done

[gêt_ɪ(t)_dʌ́n]

Verb　Conversation

Def : accomplish a task

日 : （さっさと）終わらせる

Syn : do it

e.g. : "I'll **get it done**, I promise." （ちゃんとやります。必ず）

Notes : Different from saying "I'll do my best"（頑張ります）, since doing one's best is not necessarily the same as getting the job done!　なかなか思いつかない単語ですので、実際に会話で使って覚えてゆきましょう。

---

11 topic sentence

[tɑ́:pɪ(k)_sént(ə)ns]

Noun　Academic

Def : the sentence that expresses the main idea of the paragraph

日 : トピック・センテンス

Syn : NA

e.g. : All **topic sentences** include a topic and a controlling idea. （トピックセンテンスには主題とそこで述べようとする考えが含まれます）

Notes : Topic sentences make your writing clear and easy to understand. They are also useful when speed-reading; the reader can simply read the first sentence of each paragraph to quickly understand the gist of the essay. トピックセンテンスを意識するとライティングでは意図がクリアになり、リーディングではエッセイの要点を容易につかむことができます。試してみましょう。

---

12 dignity

[dígnəti]

Noun　Academic

Def : calm behavior that makes people respect you

日 : 威厳

Syn : self-possession

e.g. : She conceded the election with **dignity** and made a memorable, moving speech.（彼女は威厳をもって選挙の敗北を認め、記憶に残る感動的なスピーチをした）

Notes : 2016 年アメリカ大統領選挙で敗れましたが、ヒラリー（Hillary Rodham Clinton）さんのスピーチは、格好良かったと思います。日本の glass ceiling を破るのは誰でしょう？

（一口アドバイス）3　Hope for the best, but prepare for the worst.

13 census

[sénsəs]

Noun　　Academic

e.g.: The government takes a **census** every 5 years. (政府は国勢調査を5年おきに実施している)

Def: an official survey of a population

日: 国勢調査

Syn: population tally

Notes: Articles about population change often refer to a specific census. 最近の日本は特にそうですが、人口の増減の際にはよくこの単語が出て来ます。他の国、例えば、US census, Canadian census などとインターネットで調べてみましょう。

---

14 "Do you have the time?"

[du ju hǽv ðə táɪm]

Other　　Conversation

e.g.: "Excuse me, but **do you have the time**?" (すみません、今何時か分かりますか)

Def: a polite way of asking the time

日: 今何時ですか？

Syn: "What time is it now?"

Notes: 外国（カナダ）の街を歩いている時によく尋ねられた文。Do you have time? (ちょっとどう？) と最初は勘違いして聞かれる度にドキドキしたのをよく覚えています。これほど冠詞の the があるなしで文の意味が異なるとは。でもカナダで腕時計を持ち歩かない人が多いのには（傘をささない人にも）驚きました。学校で習う What time is it now? はカナダ留学中一度も聞きませんでした。Do you have the time? の方が丁寧な表現です。

---

15 bilingual

[baɪlíŋgwəl]

Adjective　　Culture

Hello! / 你好。/

e.g.: Barbara is **bilingual** in English and Japanese. (バーバラは英語と日本語との二言語を使うことができる)

Def: using two languages

日: 二言語使用の

Syn: NA

Notes: All women in the English Department should consider themselves as being bilingual and using the skills that they are learning to help them understand language, culture and their future selves.　英語を専攻する学生は全員自分がバイリンガルであると気づいて、言語や文化を理解するだけでなく将来を切り拓く力にして欲しいですね。

---

16 comprehensive

[kὰːmprɪhénsɪv]

Adjective　　Academic

e.g.: Every year I have a **comprehensive** medical check. (毎年総合健康診断を受けることにしています)

Def: including everything

日: 包括的な

Syn: thorough

Notes: Other uses of this word include comprehensive insurance coverage, or a comprehensive review of an issue. そのほかにも自動車総合保険や包括的な論評・批評 (review) などにも使われます。ただし、comprehensible というと「理解可能な」という意味になりますので気をつけましょう。comprehensible input（理解可能なインプット）。

（一口アドバイス）4　Only connect.（E. M. Forster）

17

put a hold on (a library book)

[pút_ə hôuld_an_ə láɪbrəri bûk]

Verb　　Academic

Def : reserve a library book

日 : 図書館の本を予約する

Syn : reserve

e.g. : I **put a hold on** the book in the library. (図書館でその本を予約した)

Notes : 図書館で人気のある本は hold 合戦になっていたのを覚えています。reserve a book ともいうことができます。

18

convincing

[kənvínsɪŋ]

Adjective　　Academic

Def : able to make you believe that something is true

日 : 説得力のある、もっともらしい

Syn : persuasive, believable

e.g. : Kenichi gave a **convincing** performance of Hamlet. (憲一のハムレットは迫真の演技だった)

Notes : An argument, or a lie, can be convincing as well. という例文にあるように convince は、単に「説得する」だけではなく「本当にその通りだと納得させる」という意味です。

19

detect

[dɪtékt]

Verb　　Basic

Def : notice something that's not easy to see

日 : 感じ取る、見破る

Syn : notice, perceive

e.g. : I **detected** a bit of sadness in his voice. (彼の声に悲しみが潜んでいるのを感じ取った)

Notes : detective stories は「探偵小説」。アガサ・クリスティを原文で読めば英語力アップ間違いなしです。

20

seating assignment

[síːtɪŋ_əsáɪnmənt]

Noun　　TOEIC

Def : a specific seat given to one

日 : 座席指定

Syn : assigned seat(s)

e.g. : The **seating assignment** for the flight was shown on the screen. (画面に飛行機の座席指定が表示されました)

Notes : This word is used for seating at theaters as well as for modes of transportation such as trains or airplanes. 劇場だけでなく飛行機などの交通機関でもよく使われます。

(一口アドバイス) 5　Be curious, not judgmental. (Walt Whitman)

21

in the first place

[ɪn ðə fɔ́rs(t)_plèɪs]

Adverb　Academic

Def : before anything else

日 : そもそも

Syn : to begin with

e.g.: **In the first place**, what is 'intelligible English'?（「通じる英語」っていうのはそもそもどういう意味ですか）

Notes : 論文でも、会話でもそうですが、「そもそも」と話を元に戻して考えることは重要なことが多くあります。そのような際に便利な表現です。

22

hilarious

[hɪléəriəs]

Adjective　Conversation

Def : extremely funny

日 : 面白おかしい

Syn : amusing, comical

e.g.: They are my favorite comedians. They are just **hilarious**!（お気に入りのお笑いコンビです。すごく面白いよ）

Notes : All my students know the word "funny," but I never hear them say "hilarious," and native English speakers use this word a lot. 英語を話す際に funny だけでなくこちらの単語も使ってみたいですね。

23

wrinkle

[ríŋk(ə)l]

Noun　Basic

Def : a line in the skin that appears as you grow older

日 : シワ

Syn : line, crease

e.g.: My grandmother had a deep **wrinkle** between her eyebrows.（祖母の眉間には深いしわが刻まれていた）

Notes : その他、wrinkle はシャツなどの衣類でも、wrinkle in a shirt などのようによく使われます。また動詞で wrinkled shirt（しわくちゃのシャツ）のように使うこともできます。

24

make sense

[méɪ(k)_séns]

Verb　Conversation

Def : have a clear meaning

日 : 意味をなす、納得できる

Syn : be rational

e.g.: His proposal doesn't **make sense** to me.（彼の提案はおかしいと思う）

Notes : 人以外が主語となります。会話では、"That makes sense."（なるほど）などと決まった表現としても使われます。覚えておきましょう。

（一口アドバイス）6　教養のあるネイティブ・スピーカーは２万語知っている。

25

cheat

[tʃiːt]

Verb　Basic

Def : act dishonestly to gain an advantage

日 : カンニングする

Syn : deceive

e.g. : It's shameful to be caught **cheating**. (カンニングしてばれるなんてみっともない)

Notes : カンニングは一生の恥です。カンニングするくらいなら0点で落第する方がマシですね。しかしこの単語は覚えておきましょう。

26

enthusiastic

[ɪnθ(j)ùːziǽstɪk]

Adjective　Basic

Def : showing intense, eager interest or approval

日 : やる気のある，熱中している

Syn : excited

e.g. : The students are **enthusiastic** about the new project. (学生達は新しいプロジェクトにやる気を出している)

Notes : 今でもこの語を覚えた高校3年生の夏のことを覚えています。何度も舌先を歯で触れながら発音練習しました。この頃から th の発音は好きだったかもしれません。

27

hang out with

[hǽŋ_áu(t)_wɪð]

Verb　Conversation

Def : spend relaxing time with (informal)

日 : 人と遊ぶ

Syn : see

e.g. : I spent the whole summer **hanging out** at the beach **with** my friends. (夏の間ずっとビーチで友だちと遊んで過ごした)

Notes : 遊ぶという際に play を思い浮かべてしまいますが、play には友だちと遊ぶという意味はなくスポーツや音楽演奏をするという意味です。もし I play with him. というと、もてあそんでいることになってしまいますので気をつけましょう。

28

identity

[aɪdéntəti]

Noun　Culture

Def : who or what someone or something is

日 : アイデンティティ、個性、帰属意識

Syn : distinctive character, sense of belonging

e.g. : Some think being black is a big part of the hip hop artist's **identity**. (黒人であることはヒップホップ・アーティストのアイデンティティの大きな部分を占めると考える者もいる)

Notes : 普通カタカナ語で使っているように、日本語になりにくい単語です。その原因は、個人から見た場合（＝個性）と社会から見た場合（＝帰属意識）の二重の意味が含まれているからです。人間が根本的に社会的動物であることを示す言葉といえます。

(一口アドバイス) 7　Know that there is something inside you that is greater than any obstacle. (Christian Larson)

29 ship

[ʃip]

Verb　Basic

Def : transport commercially

日 : 送る

Syn : send

e.g. : Your purchase has already been **shipped**. (あなたが購入された商品はすでに発送済みです)

Notes : 荷物を送るという場合、「船」以外で送る時でも "ship" が使われます（例、shipping fee、送料）。海外のウェブサイトなどで商品を購入した場合はこのメッセージを見ることになりますので、船便か、遅くてやだな、とか思わないように。

30 obvious

[áːbviəs]

Adjective　Basic

Def : easy to recognize

日 : 明白な、わかりきった

Syn : evident, clear

Which is black?

e.g. : It is **obvious** that the play cannot be completed in so short a time. (その芝居がそんな短期間で仕上げられないことは明白だ)

Notes : obvious の発音は結構難しいです。あえてカタカナで書けば、「オブヴィアス」より「オッヴィアス」という感じです。練習しましょう。

31 argue

[áːrgjuː]

Verb　Basic

Def : give reasons in support of an idea or theory

日 : ～（正当だ）と主張する

Syn : contend

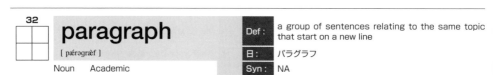

e.g. : I would **argue** that grit is the most important learner characteristic for those who want to improve their English. (やりぬく力こそが英語能力の向上に最も重要であると考えます)

Notes : 論文やレポートで 1 回は使ってみるとよいのがこの argue、自分が最も強く主張したいところで（例、I would argue [that 節]）使うと良いでしょう。意味合いは discuss と似ていますが、I discuss [that 節] とはできないので気をつけましょう。

32 paragraph

[pærəgræf]

Noun　Academic

Def : a group of sentences relating to the same topic that start on a new line

日 : パラグラフ

Syn : NA

e.g. : Organizing your essay into **paragraphs** makes it easier for the reader to follow your ideas. (エッセイのポイントをパラグラフにまとめることによってあなたの考えが分かりやすくなります)

Notes : Good paragraphs often contain one main idea, with supporting examples and a concluding sentence. パラグラフの構成はメインのアイディアがひとつ（トピックセンテンス）とそれを支える例、それにまとめとなる文です。日本語の段落とは構成が異なります。この説明にピンと来ない人は先生に詳しく説明をしてもらってください。

（一口アドバイス）8　Success consists of going from failure to failure without loss of enthusiasm. (Winston Churchill)

33 be supposed to

[bɪ səpóuz(d)_tu]

Verb　　Basic

Def : used to refer to a written or unwritten rule

日 : ～することになっている

Syn : be expected to

e.g. : You **are supposed to** be in the classroom before the class begins. （授業が始まる前に教室に入っておかなければならない）

Notes : あらゆる場面で用いられる頻出表現です。must や have to と比べてニュアンスは柔らかいですが、実質同じ内容になることが多いので注意しましょう。例文の場合、「遅刻厳禁！」という意味になります。

---

34 enroll

[ɪnróul]

Verb　　Academic

Def : register as a student

日 : 入学する、登録する

Syn : register

e.g. : Toshihisa decided to **enroll** in a basic French course. （利久は基礎フランス語講座に登録することを決めた）

Notes : roll が名簿や出席簿ということがわかれば、enroll はわかりやすいです。ほかにもロールケーキの roll など roll は多くの意味があります。

---

35 cut class

[kʌ̀(t)_klǽs]

Verb　　Basic

Def : miss class without permission

日 : （授業を）さぼる

Syn : skip class

e.g. : I'll **cut classes** and watch movies. （授業をサボって映画を見てやろう）

Notes : 高校では習わない単語ですね。その他にも授業がないと言う際に、"Class won't meet." "There's no class." などと表現することも覚えておくといいですね。

---

36 "How do you like ～ ? "

[hàu du ju láik]

Other　　Conversation

Def : What kind of/style of ～ do you like?

日 : ～はどうなさいますか、どう思いますか

Syn : "How do you take～?"

e.g. : "**How do you like** your coffee?" （コーヒーはどうなさいますか [砂糖とクリームはどうなさいますか]）。

Notes : 間違った訳を見かけることがあります。「どのように好きですか」などとは決して訳さないようにしましょう。「どうしましょう」と好みを聞いているだけですよ。

（一口アドバイス）9　歌や映画でお気に入りのフレーズを覚えましょう。

37 incentive

[ɪnséntɪv]

Noun　TOEIC

Def : something that encourages you to do something

日 : 刺激（報酬）

Syn : impetus

e.g. : Getting high scores would be an **incentive** to keep studying.（高得点を取ったら、勉強を続けようという気になる）

Notes : An incentive is something offered as a reward, while most motivation comes from within. Motivation と違って「報酬」とか「利益」という文脈で使うことが多いです。「インセンティブ」として日本語としても使われることが多くなりました。皆さんの英語上達のためには、何が incentive や motivation になっているのでしょう。

38 hectic

[héktɪk]

Adjective　Conversation

Def : extremely busy

日 : 多忙な

Syn : chaotic

e.g. : I had a **hectic** day today!（今日は超多忙な一日だった）

Notes : busy よりもっと慌ただしく大騒ぎしている感じです。人に使用することはないので要注意。"I was hectic." ではなく "Things were hectic." などとなります。

39 participant

[pɑːrtísəpənt]

Noun　Linguistics

Def : someone who takes part in an activity

日 : 参加者

Syn : subject

e.g. : Professor Edasawa recruited 100 college students as **participants** in her study.（枝澤教授は研究のために100 名の大学生を参加者として集めた）

Notes : 1980 年代ころまでは、subjects（被験者）という言葉を使っていましたが、人を物のように扱うのは不適切ということで、現在では質問紙（アンケート）を配布する場合にも回答してくれる人は participants（調査への参加者）という言葉で表すことになっています。もちろん動詞形は participate (in)。

40 concluding sentence

[kənklúːdɪŋ sént(ə)ns]

Noun　Academic

Def : the final sentence of a paragraph

日 : パラグラフの締めの文

Syn : conclusion

e.g. : A **concluding sentence** often restates the ideas of the topic sentence.（パラグラフの最後の文はトピックセンテンスの趣旨をもう一度述べることが多い）

Notes : Paragraphs that do not have a concluding sentence seem incomplete. パラグラフの締めの文がないと不完全な印象を与えることがありますので気をつけましょう。

（一口アドバイス）10　Wonder is the beginning of wisdom.

41 "Have a go."

[hǽv_ə góu]

Other　Conversation

Def : make an attempt (UK)

日 : やってみてください！

Syn : "Give it a try."

e.g. : "Don't worry. Just **have a go**."（心配しないで。まずやってみて下さい）

Notes : It is a nice friendly way of inviting someone to try something. 会話でそのまま使えます。まずは友だちに言ってみましょう。

---

42 fabulous

[fǽbjələs]

Adjective　Basic

Def : extremely good

日 : 途方もない、ものすごい

Syn : extraordinary, wonderful

e.g. : The billionaire held a **fabulous** party at his mansion.（その億万長者は豪邸ですごいパーティを開いた）

Notes : 次の表現も有名です。"Never miss an opportunity to be fabulous."（光り輝くチャンスを逃すな）Tina Seelig, Ph.D. Stanford School of Engineering (https://www.youtube.com/watch?v=bf8a3hHsxNQ)

---

43 proficient

[prəfíʃənt]

Adjective　Linguistics

Def : fully trained and skillful

日 : 能力の高い

Syn : able, capable

e.g. : She is **proficient** in French.（彼女はフランス語がよくできる）

Notes : Native English speakers as well as learners of English tend to overuse the word "good." This is one substitute that sounds much more impressive. good の代わりに使ってみましょう。発音では強勢の位置に注意しましょう。名詞形は proficiency (English proficiency、英語能力) です。

---

44 spouse

[spáus]

Noun　Basic

Def : a husband or wife

日 : 配偶者

Syn : a husband or wife

e.g. : He's Japanese and his **spouse** is French.（彼は日本国籍で、奥さんはフランス人です）

Notes : 夫、妻両方を含む便利な単語です。sibling の欄（p. 13）も参照して下さい。昔は、パーティーなどに、You can bring your spouse. と書かれていましたが、最近では spouse の代わりに partner が使われるようです（特に UK で）。

45

"What a waste!"

[wɑ́t̮ə wéɪst]

Other　　Conversation

Def : expresses disappointment at the inefficient use of something

日 : もったいない

Syn : "That's wasteful."

e.g. : "Don't throw it away! **What a waste!**" (捨てないで！もったいない)

Notes : Some Japanese people think "mottainai" is a uniquely Japanese idea. Of course it isn't! Different languages have their own equivalents. "What a waste!" or "How wasteful" are English versions.「もったいない」に対応する英語はあるのですね。ただ一方で mottainai を英語で表しにくいのも事実ですね。言葉の面白いところです。

46

in advance

[ɪn̮ədvǽns]

Adverb　　Academic

Def : before a particular time

日 : 事前に

Syn : beforehand

e.g. : When you are absent from this class, you need to email me **in advance**, not afterward. (授業を欠席するときには事後でなく、事前にメールで知らせてください)

Notes : 大学では締めきり (deadline, due date) など時間に関する表現を使うことが多くあります。突然の病気などで欠席ということもありますが、できる限り先生には連絡をするといいですね。もっともメールは丁寧に書くように気をつけましょう。また自分の名前やどの授業の欠席なのかも明記することが重要です。当たり前ですが。

47

LGBTQ

[él dʒíː bíː tíː kjúː]

Adjective　　Culture

Def : an acronym for "lesbian, gay, bisexual, transgender and queer"

日 : 性的少数者

Syn : lesbian, gay, bisexual, transgender

e.g. : Last week the local **LGBTQ** community held a parade in my neighborhood. (先週、性的少数者グループによるパレードがうちの近所で行われた)

Notes : This acronym has become standard usage, and its meaning should be known by all English learners. LGBTQ として日本の新聞紙上でもよく見かけるようになりました。レインボーをシンボルに pride parade が全世界で開催されています。

48

app

[ǽp]

Noun　　Current

Def : an application for a mobile device

日 : 携帯のアプリ

Syn : NA

e.g. : I downloaded a great **app** for my iPhone from the App Store. (インターネットからアイフォン用にいいアプリをダウンロードした)

Notes : 日本語訳はアプリですが英語で「アプリ」と言わないように気をつけましょう。発音は /æp/ です。

(一口アドバイス) 12　A book that is shut is but a block. (Thomas Fuller)

49

female

[fíːmeɪl]

Adjective　Academic

Def : of being a woman or a member of the sex that can give birth

日 : 女性の、雌の

Syn : women's

e.g. : The number of **female** entrepreneurs is increasing.（女性の起業家が増えている）

Notes : 「女性の」という時、women's を使いがちですが、female を知っていると便利。合わせて male（男性の、雄の）も覚えたいですね。

50

conditions

[kəndíʃnz]

Noun　Academic

Def : things that must be done before something else can happen

日 : 条件

Syn : requirements

e.g. : The University of Toronto offered Kumiko a **conditional** admission.（久美子さんは条件付きでトロント大学に入学を許可された）

Notes : 海外の大学（院）の合格には、conditional（条件付き）というケースがあります。例えば、TOEFL のスコアが十分でないなどもそのケース。私の場合はカナダの大学院に合格した際、日本の大学（学部）の卒業証書（原本）を持参するという condition（条件）が付いていました。実際に admission office で見せたけれど、日本語で書いてある内容を理解しているようには見えませんでした。その他、保険などで terms and conditions（契約条件）という用語としても使われます。

51

universal

[jùːnəvə́ːrs(ə)l]

Adjective　Literature

Def : relating to everyone

日 : 普遍的

Syn : worldwide

e.g. : The need to make friends and to be loved is **universal**.（友だちが欲しい、誰かに愛されたいという欲求は普遍的である）

Notes : This is a word you might use to talk about all humanity and what connects us all. 人類や我々全てに関わる事を述べる際に使われる言葉ですね。

52

sibling

[síblɪŋ]

Noun　Basic

Def : a sister or brother

日 : 兄弟姉妹

Syn : a sister or brother

e.g. : "Do you have any **siblings**?"（兄弟はいますか？）"Yes, I have a brother and a sister."（弟と姉がいます）

Notes : 日本人は大抵 "Do you have any brothers or sisters?" といいますが、兄弟姉妹あわせていうことのできる便利な単語です。同様の単語に spouse（配偶者）があります。この場合、夫、妻、両方を含むことができます。spouse（p. 11）も参照してください。

（一口アドバイス）13　Life moves pretty fast. If you don't stop and look around once in a while, you could miss it. (Ferris, *Ferris Bueller's Day Off*)

— 15 —

53

tidy

[táɪdi]

Adjective　Basic

Def : arranged in an orderly way

日 : きちんとした

Syn : neat

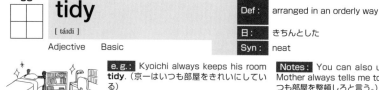

e. g. : Kyoichi always keeps his room **tidy**. (京一はいつも部屋をきれいにしている)

Notes : You can also use this word as a verb: Mother always tells me to tidy up my room. (母はいつも部屋を整頓しろと言う。)「きちんとする」という意味の動詞にもなります。似たような動詞に "Pick up this room!"、"Clean up this room!" などがあります。

54

coincidence

[kouínsədəns]

Noun　Academic

Def : two events happening in the same way or at the same time by chance

日 : 偶然

Syn : fluke

e. g. : It was a pure **coincidence** that my sister and I both married tennis players. (私と妹が両方ともテニス選手と結婚したのは単なる偶然だった)

Notes : This word can be used to express an incident when two or more things happen at the same time, especially when it is not expected or surprising.

55

"Don't you dare!"

[dòuntʃu déər]

Other　Conversation

Def : a strong warning not to do something

日 : やめなさい！

Syn : "Don't even think about it!"

e. g. : "Cut classes and watch movies? **Don't you dare!**"（授業をサボって映画を見るなんて、とんでもない！）

Notes : 辞書で dare を調べると「勇気をもって〜する」のようなポジティブな意味が最初にくるかもしれませんが、会話表現では例文のような状況が多いです。大げんか寸前の言葉なので、現実世界で "How dare you!" とかを耳にしたら要注意！

56

part time

[pá:r(t)_tàɪm]

Adverb　Conversation

Def : for only part of the usual workday or week

日 : アルバイトで

Syn : NA

e. g. : Midori started to work at the bank **part time** when her child entered first grade. (こどもが小学校に行き始めてから、ミドリさんが銀行でパートで働き始めた)

Notes : よく使う語彙ですが、What are you going to do this weekend?（今週末の予定は）に対する回答としては、I'm going to work. と答えると（今週末は）アルバイトをする予定、という意味に、I have a [part-time] job. というと、（最近週末は）アルバイトをしています、という意味になります。この場合、大学生なので仕事がアルバイトであることは自明なので、part-time を付けなくても OK、また逆に、例文のように I work part-time. とすることも可能です。

(一口アドバイス) 14　As you read, pay attention to the words that are used with other words.

57

"I couldn't agree with you more."

[aɪ kûdnt̬_əgríː wið_ju mɔ́ːr]

Other　　Conversation

Def : used to express complete agreement

日 : 全面的に賛成です、まったく同感です

Syn : I completely agree with you.

e.g. : "Joe's Pizza is the best pizzaria around here, you say? **I couldn't agree with you more.**" (ジョーズ・ピッツァがこの辺で一番のピザ屋だって？本当にそうだよね)

Notes : しようたってこれ以上強くは賛成できない、したがって、最上級の賛成、ということです。否定文なのに肯定の意味で混乱しそうですが、"(The weather) couldn't be better" のように英語にはよくあるタイプの表現です。

58

supporting sentence

[səpɔ́ːrtɪŋ sént(ə)ns]

Noun　　Academic

Def : a sentence that provides details to support the topic

日 : 支持文

Syn : NA

e.g. : Supporting sentences develop and add detail to the main idea of a paragraph as stated in the topic sentence. (支持文はトピックセンテンスで述べられた段落の主題を発展させたり細目を加えたりします)

Notes : Supporting sentences commonly include examples, details, and reasons.　支持文の特徴として、例、詳細な記述、理由などが含まれます。

59

genuine

[dʒénjuɪn]

Adjective　　Basic

Def : not false or copied

日 : 本格的、本当の、本物の

Syn : real, authentic

e.g. : 1) She is such a **genuine** person. She is never fake. (彼女は本当に誠実なひとです。ウソがありません)
2) He prides himself on having a **genuine** Picasso. (彼は本物のピカソの絵をもっていることを自慢している)

Notes : A useful word that can be used to talk about people or things. For people it means "sincere" and for things it means "real." "Authentic" can also be used for both. 人に対しても物についても使うことができる役に立つ単語です。authentic も同様に使うことができます。

60

reimburse

[r̀iːmbə́ːrs]

Verb　　TOEIC

Def : pay back money

日 : 払い戻す

Syn : repay

e.g. : The university will **reimburse** students for the TOEIC fees. (大学はTOEIC テスト受験料を学生に払い戻すだろう)

Notes : TOEIC テストでもよく出題される単語です。get reimbursed で払い戻される、という意味になります。あわせて覚えておきましょう。

（一口アドバイス）15　論文は一日一文、語彙は一日五語。

61

"After you."
[ǽftər júː]

Other　Conversation

Def : used to suggest for someone to go ahead of you

日： お先にどうぞ

Syn : "You can go first."

e.g.: "Oh, **after you**. I'm in no hurry."
（お先にどうぞ。こっちは急ぎじゃないんで）

Notes： ドアから入るとき、列に並ぶとき、どちらが先かなとなるときがありますね。その場合、"After you." で相手にゆずることができればオシャレです。逆に言われたときは下手に遠慮しないで、好意を受けることにしましょう。

62

insurance
[ɪnʃúərəns]

Noun　TOEIC

Def : promise of payment in the case of a loss

日： 保険

Syn : coverage

e.g.: When you rent a car, be sure to purchase **insurance**. （車を借りる際には保険に入るのをお忘れなく）

Notes： 強勢の位置に注意しましょう。海外ではレンタカーを借りる際、保険をどうしようか、と考えるケースが多いです（健康保険は大学の授業料に組み込まれていることが多い）。車の保険って結構高いけれどケチらないように（full coverage）したいですね。

63

brilliant
[bríljənt]

Adjective　Basic

Def : 1. extremely intelligent or skillful
2. Fantastic! (UK)

日： 天才的、すごい

Syn : 1. brainy　　2. wonderful! (UK)

e.g.: 1. Einstein had a **brilliant** mind. （アインシュタインは天才的な頭脳を持っていた）
2. "You're going to Russia? **Brilliant**!" （ロシアに行くの？ステキ！）

Notes： A useful word with different nuances depending on the context. 複数の意味がありますが、学生は使えていないですね。使ってみましょう！

64

text
[tékst]

Verb　Current

Def : send a written message via an SMS application from a mobile phone

日： （携帯電話、スマートフォンで）メールする

Syn : send an SMS message

e.g.: My best friend's boyfriend **texted** me that he loves me! （親友の彼氏がメール送ってきてさ、私が好きになっちゃっただって！）

Notes： テクノロジーの発展で単語に新しい用法が生まれることがあります。text は名詞ではおなじみですが、携帯機器の普及で動詞としても頻用されるようになりました。メール・サービスは英語では SMS (short message service) です。

（一口アドバイス）16　Education is the kindling of a flame, not the filling of a vessel.

65

literary

[lítərèri]

Adjective   Literature

Def : connected with literature

日 : 文学の、文学的

Syn : NA

e.g. : **Literary** translation is extremely challenging. （文学作品の翻訳は極めて難しい）

Notes : Useful for talking about books and writing. A great book is a literary gem; a great writer is someone with literary genius. 教養の中核をなすといわれる文学、言葉にも literary gem（文学の宝石）、literary genius（文豪）などいろいろな語があります。あわせて覚えておきましょう。

66

contribute to

[kəntríbju:(t)_tu]

Verb   Academic

Def : be a factor in

日 : 一因となる

Syn : help to cause or bring about

e.g. : Cutting rainforests for farming also **contributes** to global warming. （農地をつくるための熱帯雨林伐採も現在の地球温暖化の原因のひとつである）

Notes : contribute を「貢献する」と記憶している人も多いようですが、この語は悪い結果に関連しても使うので、「貢献」だとおかしくなる場合もあります。社会問題について書いてある場合、その「一因となっている」と読みましょう。

67

ambiguous

[æmbígjuəs]

Adjective   Basic

Def : open to more than one interpretation

日 : 曖昧な

Syn : vague

e.g. : The boy's answer was so **ambiguous** that I couldn't tell what he meant. （その子の答えは非常に曖昧だったので、何を言いたいのか分からなかった）

Notes : Strictly speaking, "ambiguous" means "having more than one meaning," while "vague" means "uncertain," "unfocused." 名詞形は ambiguity です。これもよく使われるので、一緒に覚えておきましょう。

68

signature

[sígnətʃər]

Noun   Basic

Def : your name written in your own handwriting

日 : サイン

Syn : autograph

e.g. : I needed his **signature** on the contract. （契約書では彼のサインが必要だった）

Notes : Notice this word is not "sign" in English! "Sign" is used only as a verb: "Please sign on the dotted line." A famous person's signature is an "autograph." 日本語のサインは英語では動詞なので注意しましょう。ちなみに有名人のサインは autograph です。

（一口アドバイス）17　次の世代はもっとちゃんとやってくれる。（Margaret Drabble）

69 figure of speech

[fɪɡjər_əv spíːtʃ]

Noun　Linguistics

Def : words used together to mean something different from their usual sense

日 : 修辞的表現、言葉の綾

Syn : figurative language

e. g.: Metaphors, similes, and personification are different kinds of **figures of speech**. (隠喩・直喩・擬人化は修辞的表現法に当たる)

Notes : Every language has imaginative figures of speech that make learning fun. 確かに「たとえ」はどの言語にも豊富にありますね。日本語では「のどから手が出るほどほしい」「へそで茶を沸かす」、また絵のような as cool as a cucumber は代表的な figures of speech です。

---

70 pastime

[pǽstàɪm]

Noun　Basic

Def : an activity that you enjoy doing when you are not working

日 : 娯楽、ひまつぶし

Syn : recreation

e. g.: My favorite **pastime** is strolling along the Kamo River. (鴨川のほとりを散歩することが私の趣味です)

Notes : Hobby and pastime are not the same! It sounds strange to say your hobby is "shopping," for example. A hobby is something like photography or hula dancing, something that requires significant skill or knowledge and not everyone can do. 日本語の趣味はこの "pastime" に近いですね。「趣味は寝ること」ですは日本語では OK でも英語では変な感じがします。

---

71 book (a table, a seat)

[búk]

Verb　Conversation

Def : reserve

日 : 予約する

Syn : make a reservation

e. g.: I **booked** the restaurant for dinner on your birthday. (誕生日のお祝いにあのレストランを予約しておいたよ)

Notes : 予約をするという際、真っ先に reserve が浮かんでくると思います。I would like to reserve a table for two. でも問題ありませんが、実際の会話では book の動詞形が使われることが多くあります。但し、大学の先生やお医者さんの場合には make an appointment を使います。一度電話でレストランの予約をしてみましょう。

---

72 mansion

[mǽnʃən]

Noun　Basic

Def : a large, expensive house

日 : 大邸宅

Syn : palace

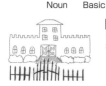

e. g.: Scott is a billionaire and lives in a **mansion** in Seattle. (スコットは億万長者でシアトルの大邸宅に住んでいる)

Notes : 日本語の「マンション」とは大違いの言葉です。日本で言うマンションは apartment, flat (UK)、または condominium に相当する。 "Where do you live?" と聞かれたら "In a mansion." ではなく "In an apartment." です。

(一口アドバイス) 18　If way to the better that be, it exacts a full look at the worst. (Thomas Hardy)

73 aspire

[əspáɪər]

Verb　Basic

Def : strongly want to do or become something

日 : 熱望する、大志を抱く

Syn : desire, dream of

e.g. : The young scientist **aspires** to find a cure for cancer someday. (若き科学者は、いつかがんの治療法を見つけ出すことを志している)

Notes : 名詞形は aspiration（大志、向上心）、ambition に似ていますね。

---

74 "Break a leg!"

[brêɪk‿ə lég]

Other　Conversation

Def : used to wish someone good luck, especially before a performance

日 : 成功を祈っています！

Syn : "Good luck!"

e.g. : Jannet said, "**Break a leg!**" before I went on stage. (舞台の前に、ジャネットに「成功を祈る」と励ましてもらった)

Notes : 演劇や歌、ダンスなどのパフォーマンスをする人を励ます言葉です。「足を折れ」という理由は、一説には舞台関係者の間で、"Good luck" というと反対に bad luck を引き寄せてしまうという迷信があるので、良い結果が出るようわざと悪いことを口にするとか。

---

75 roller coaster

[róulər kòustər]

Noun　Conversation

Def : a ride or experience filled with strong ups and downs

日 : ジェット・コースター

Syn : NA

e.g. : We are looking forward to riding on a **roller coaster**. (ジェットコースターに乗るのを私たちは楽しみにしている)

Notes : ジェット・コースターという言葉は和製英語です。その他、観覧車は "Ferris wheel"、回転木馬が "merry-go-round" です。比喩的使い方も多いです。たとえば Love is a roller coaster. のように使えます。

---

76 initiate

[ɪníʃièɪt]

Verb　Basic

Def : cause something to begin（formal）

日 : 始める

Syn : launch

e.g. : Professor Nakajima **initiated** a new project. (中島教授は新しいプロジェクトを始めた)

Notes : 始めるという単語には様々な単語がありますが、begin, start 以外の表現方法も覚えておきたいですね。この単語から派生した語として、initiative（名詞：主導権）などがあります。

（一口アドバイス）19　But I have promises to keep, and miles to go before I sleep. (Robert Frost)

77 lingua franca

[líŋgwə frǽŋkə]

Noun　Linguistics

Def : a common language used by speakers of various languages

日 : 共通語

Syn : common language

e. g. : English is the most widespread **lingua franca** in the world today. （英語は現在最も一般的な世界の共通言語だ）

Notes : Although English is known to be the lingua franca of the world today, that does not mean that there is only one type of English; Benglish (Bengali and English) and Finglish (Finnish and English) are some of the variants of the language. 英語が共通語だからといって、ひとつの英語だけでなく World Englishes としていろいろな英語が使われています。

78 spontaneous

[spɑːntéɪnɪəs]

Adjective　Basic

Def : happening in a natural way without being forced

日 : 自発的な、自然発生的な

Syn : unplanned, unforced, impulsive

e. g. : When she appeared on the stage, **spontaneous** applause broke out from the audience. （彼女が登場すると、観客から自然に拍手がわき起った）

Notes : William Wordsworth の詩 （*Lyrical Ballads* の序文） に、 "Poetry is the spontaneous overflow of powerful feelings" （詩とは感情の自然な発露である） という有名な一節がありますね。

79 intelligible

[ɪntélɪdʒəb(ə)l]

Adjective　Linguistics

Def : clear enough to be understood

日 : 理解できる

Syn : comprehensible

e. g. : The most important thing in English pronunciation is being **intelligible**. （英語の発音で一番大切なことは通じることです）

Notes : 日本人が英語を学ぶ理由、それは世界共通語 （English as a global lingua franca: EGLF） としての英語だからでしょう。ネイティブ・スピーカーのような英語は格好いいし、それを目標にしてもいいです。でもまず EGLF として英語を使う場合、native-like ではなくて、理解可能な英語からスタートしましょう。話しているうちに上手くなりいつの日にか英語の expert になれますよ。

80 allowance

[əláʊəns]

Noun　TOEIC

Def : a small amount of money given regularly to someone

日 : お小遣い、手当て

Syn : payment

e. g. : Some children receive a monthly **allowance** if they help with household chores. （子供が家事を手伝えば、お小遣いがもらえる家庭もある）

Notes : When I was young, my siblings and I received a monthly allowance of 2 dollars for helping my mother around the house. 「お小遣い」という意味から、例えばキャビンアテンダントが国際線で海外に滞在する際の 「手当」 など幅広く使われます。

（一口アドバイス）20　You will never progress, if you practice only occasionally, only reluctantly.

81

a ride

[ə ráɪd]

Noun   Conversation

Def : a short journey in a vehicle, especially a car

日 : （乗り物に）乗ること、乗せること

Syn : a lift

e.g. : "Do you want **a ride** to the station?"（駅まで乗せてあげましょうか？）

Notes : There is no direct noun equivalent in Japanese, but it is extremely common in English and easy to use. 日本語に直訳できませんが、英語ではよく使われる表現なので覚えておきたいです。

82

competent

[kάːmpət(ə)nt]

Adjective   Academic

Def : able to do something well

日 : 能力のある

Syn : skilled

e.g. : It took me years of practice to become **competent** at kendo. （剣道に秀でるようになるまで長年の練習を要した）

Notes : The antonym, "incompetent," is insulting, so be careful. この単語の反意語である incompetent の使用には十分気をつけましょう。

83

immigrant

[ímɪɡrənt]

Noun   Culture

Def : someone who comes to live in a different country

日 : 移民

Syn : settler, incomer (UK), migrant

e.g. : Japanese **immigrants** have contributed greatly to the culture of Hawaii. （日系移民がハワイの文化に多大な貢献をしてきました）

Notes : 国際情勢を知るのに重要な単語です。emigrant というと「外国への移民」をさします。それぞれの動詞は immigrate, emigrate となります。

84

discriminate

[dɪskrímənèɪt]

Verb   Academic

Def : treat a category of people unfairly

日 : 差別する、区別する

Syn : be biased, prejudiced

e.g. : They **discriminated** against a minority group. （彼らは少数派を差別した）

Notes : discriminate against 〜で「〜を差別する」という表現になります。

（一口アドバイス）21　I promise not to be a procrastinator!

85 paraphrase

[pǽrəfrèɪz]

Verb   Academic

Def : restate something using different words

日 : 違う言葉で言い換える

Syn : reword

e.g.: I don't understand this sentence. Could you **paraphrase** it for me? (この文、内容がよくわからないよ。わかりやすく言い直してくれる？)

Notes : Paraphrasing is a key skill in academic writing. When you write a paper, you cannot always copy the words from sources that you use directly. You need to use your own words. 短い文章を分かりやすく説明などを加えて「パラフレーズ」することができます。お気に入りの歌の歌詞をパラフレーズして、人に伝えてみましょう。

---

86 "Don't hold back."

[dôun(t)_hôul(d)_bǽk]

Other   Conversation

Def : Don't hesitate (from shyness, etc).

日 : 遠慮しないでください

Syn : "Don't be shy. Speak up."

e.g.: "If you have any questions, please **don't hold back**." (質問があればご自由にどうぞ)

Notes : If you are teaching a class or holding a meeting and you want people to feel able to ask questions or comment, this is a useful expression. 「日本人は質問しない」といわれていますが、みなが質問しやすい温かい雰囲気をつくることは大切ですね。授業でも、会議でも、どこでも。

---

87 24/7

[twénti fɔ́:r sév(ə)n]

Adverb   Conversation

Def : 24 hours a day, 7 days a week

日 : 四六時中

Syn : all the time

e.g.: That restaurant is open **24/7**. (そのレストランは年中無休です)

Notes : "24/7" と数字で書きます。一日24時間、一週間7日ずっと、ということです。実際にはそんなことは、無休で24時間営業の店舗以外にはないでしょうが、誇張表現としてよく使われます。"I'm thinking about you 24/7, my love." とか・・・。

---

88 lyrics

[lírɪks]

Noun   Literature

Def : the words of a song

日 : 歌詞

Syn : words

e.g.: I love that song's **lyrics**. They really move me. (その歌の歌詞はいいなあ。グッとくるよ)

Notes : Useful for talking about music. インターネットで歌詞検索をする場合にはこの単語と歌の題名をいれましょう。例えば、Imagine lyrics で、ジョン・レノンの「イマジン」の歌詞を素早く探すことができます。また形容詞の lyrical (抒情的) もあわせて覚えておきましょう。

（一口アドバイス）22　雲はときどき竜のように見えるけど、雲って実態のない靄。でも、人間はそんなものを恐れる。(William Shakespeare)

89

grit

[grít]

Noun   Academic

Def : mental toughness and courage

日 : やり抜く力

Syn : perseverance

e.g. : You need to have **grit** if you want to succeed in this competitive world. (この競争社会で成功しようと思ったらやり抜く力を持たなければならない)

Notes : Grit goes hand in hand with success. At times, we give up too easily and forget that the risks and mistakes we experience are helping us to become stronger and actually preparing us to succeed. 失敗は次の成功への準備となることを覚えてやり抜く力をつけてゆきたいですね。

90

subtitle

[sʌ́(b)tàɪt(ə)l]

Noun   Communication

Def : written translation of dialogue on a screen

日 : 字幕

Syn : caption

e.g. : US filmgoers generally prefer dubbed foreign films to those with **subtitles**. (アメリカでは字幕付き映画より吹き替えのほうが人気があるようだ)

Notes : Studying with subtitles is an excellent way to study English. Watch the same scene of a TV drama or film with English subtitles, then Japanese subtitles, then no subtitles. Repeat. 字幕を使った英語学習法も是非実践してみて下さい。

91

run into

[rʌ́n_ɪntu]

Verb   Conversation

Def : meet someone you know by chance

日 : 偶然出会う

Syn : bump into

e.g. : I **ran into** my high school English teacher yesterday. (昨日バッタリと高校時代にお世話になった英語の先生に出会った)

Notes : 例えば文学作品では、「I ran into my ex-boy-friend yesterday.」のような文が出てくることがありますが、昔、この文を「昨日、元彼の胸の中に飛び込んだ」と訳した友人がいました。キケンな雰囲気がでてしまう誤訳ですね。

92

"Negative."

[négətɪv]

Other   Conversation

Def : not possible, that's wrong, that doesn't exist

日 : 駄目、無理

Syn : "No."

e.g. : "Can you see Mt. Fuji from there?" "**Negative**, it's cloudy today." (そこから富士山見える？ ダメだね、今日は曇りだから)

Notes : "No." の他にも、質問に否定で答える仕方はあります。"No way!" "Absolutely not." "Impossible." など。表現にバラエティをもたせるために色々使ってみましょう。"Negative" は元は軍隊用語で、日常に使うとちょっとユーモラスです。

(一口アドバイス) 23　Someday everything will make perfect sense.

93

hand in hand

[hǽnd_ɪn_hǽnd]

Adverb　Basic

Def : 1. holding hands
2. closely connected

日 : 手に手を取って

Syn : holding hands

e.g. : I saw Meg walking **hand in hand** with her little son. （メグが坊やと手をつないで歩いているのを目にした）

Notes : ミルトン（John Milton）の『失楽園』(*Paradise Lost*) では、アダムとイヴが楽園の東の門から手に手を取って（hand in hand）歩み出す姿が、最終場面として描かれています。実際に本を手にとって読んでみましょう。尚、「伴う」という意味もあります。

94

script

[skrípt]

Noun　Communication

Def : the words of a movie, play, or speech

日 : 台本

Syn : screenplay

e.g. : After we finish casting, I will give you the **script**. （配役が終わったら、台本を渡しますね）

Notes : シェイクスピア・プロダクションをはじめ演劇の世界ではなくてはならない単語ですね。movie script というと映画の台本になります。

95

accommodation

[əkɑ̀mədéɪʃən]

Noun　TOEIC

Def : a room or rooms where someone stays when traveling

日 : 宿泊施設

Syn : a place to stay

e.g. : Finding **accommodation** during the Gion Festival in Kyoto is difficult. （祇園祭の間は宿を見つけるのが難しい）

Notes : This is a word often used in the travel and hospitality industry. 旅行や観光業界でよく使う言葉です。

96

"Hi, guys."

[hâɪ gáɪz]

Other　Conversation

Def : informal greeting to a group of people

日 : やあ、みんな

Syn : "Hello, everyone."

e.g. : "**Hi, guys**. Where's Melissa? Hasn't she arrived yet?" （やあ、みんな。メリッサは？まだ来てないの？）

Notes : 複数の親しい人たちがいる場所に入るときに使います。"guy" は「男」という意味ですが、その場に女性だけしかいない場合でも使えるようです。アメリカのTVドラマで頻出の表現です。

---

97 consonant

[kάːnsənənt]

Noun　Linguistics

Def : a speech sound that is not a vowel

日 : 子音

Syn : NA

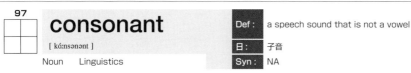

e.g. : Please pronounce **consonants** clearly. (子音をハッキリと発音しましょう)

Notes : Lots of students seem to know the word "vowel," but nobody seems to know the word "consonant." 母音に比べて子音の印象は確かに薄いですね。

---

98 obligation

[ὰːblɪgéɪʃən]

Noun　Academic

Def : something that you must do

日 : 義務

Syn : duty

e.g. : Your final **obligation** in this course is to give a presentation. (みなさんがこのコースですべきことはあとひとつ、プレゼンテーションをすることです)

Notes : 大学に入学してゼミの先生からこの obligation という単語を聞いた情景をいまも覚えています。「大学生がすべきこと」のように個別で具体的な義務の際に obligation を使うのに対して、一般的な義務については duty、法的な義務を強調する際には liability を使い分けます。

---

99 ASAP

[éɪ ès èɪ píː]

Adverb　Conversation

Def : as soon as possible

日 : 早急に

Syn : immediately

e.g. : You know, the deadline was yesterday. Send the draft **ASAP**. (わかってると思うけど、締め切りは昨日ね。すぐに原稿送って)

Notes : as soon as possible の略。略して短くした分だけ、急ぎのニュアンスが強く感じられます。ちなみに、as soon as you can になると、「そちらの都合のつくかぎりで出来るだけ早く」と、ちょっと余裕を与える表現になります。

---

100 procrastinator

[prəkrǽstɪnèɪtər]

Noun　Academic

Def : someone who keeps delaying things that must be done

日 : ものごとを先延ばしする人

Syn : procrastinate (v): put off, delay, postpone

e.g. : I don't want to be a **procrastinator** in anything. (何事に関しても先延ばしをする人にはなりたくないです)

Notes : "I hate people who do things at the last minute." と言ったら "Oh, you mean 'procrastinators.'" と、一語で表現できる語があることに感動したのを覚えています。

(一口アドバイス) 25　楽しくない勉強は続かない。

Part 2

Discovery

And one day
she discovered
that she was fierce,
and strong
and full of fire,
and that not even
she could
hold herself back
because her passion
burned brighter
than her fears
(Mark Anthony, 2016)

Anthony, M. (2016). *The beautiful truth*. Create Space Independent Publishing Platform.

101 point of view

[pɔ́ɪnt_ə(v)_vjúː]

Noun   Literature

Def : the way people think about something

日 : 視点

Syn : viewpoint, opinion, angle, perspective

e.g. : The short story alternates between two **points of view**: the father's and the son's. (この短編小説は二つの視点、父親と息子の視点を交互に用いている)

Notes : 授業では「何か "point of view" を決めて分析しなさい」と学生のみなさんによく言っています。フィクションを読む際に、視点がどのように設定されているかは非常に重要です。同じ出来事でもどの立場から描くかによって、読者に何が伝わるかが大きく変わります。"point of view" は使い方によっては、「意見」や「立場」の意味にもなります。小説を分析するときにもよく使う言葉です。

102 humble

[hʌmb(ə)l]

Adjective   Literature

Def : not boastful, not bragging about oneself

日 : 謙虚な

Syn : modest

e.g. : Bill's friends praise him for his warm personality and **humble** attitude. (ビルの友人は、彼の温かな人柄と謙虚な態度をほめる)

Notes : 反対語は "proud" です。キリスト教では、傲慢 (pride) はサタンにつながる悪徳、謙虚 (humility) はイエスにつながる美徳とされます。発音に注意しましょう。

103 disguise

[dɪsɡáɪz]

Verb   Basic

Def : change someone's appearance so that it is unrecognizable

日 : 変装する

Syn : camouflage, mask

e.g. : In the play, the heroine **disguises** herself as a man. (劇中でヒロインは男装をする)

Notes : 「変装」はシェイクスピア劇のキーワードの一つ。ヒロインが男装する作品も多く見られます。当時、女役は変声期前の少年俳優が演じていたので、ヒロインの男装は複雑な舞台効果をもたらしたと考えられます。

104 almost all

[ɔ́ːlmoust_ɔ́ːl]

Other   Basic

Def : close to 100%

日 : ほとんど

Syn : nearly all

e.g. : **Almost all** the college students in Japan work part-time. (日本のほとんどの大学生がアルバイトをしている)

Notes : 簡単な単語ですが、"Almost college students …" といった誤用が多く見られます。"Most college students … " とするか、例文のように all をつけて使う用法が正解です。

（一口アドバイス）26　Make learning part of your habit, and habit will become part of your learning.

105 "It tastes nice."

[ɪ(t)_têɪsts náɪs]

Other　Basic

Def : very good to eat or drink

日 : 美味しい

Syn : delicious, yum

e. g. : "Does it **taste nice**?" "Yes, very nice." (美味しい？とっても美味しいよ)

Notes : Many Japanese speakers of English say, "Taste is nice" but we don't say that. We use the verb: it tastes nice. 美味しいという際の言い方を覚えておきましょう。

---

106 vital

[váɪt(ə)l]

Adjective　Basic

Def : very important

日 : きわめて重要な、活気のある

Syn : essential, critical

e. g. : Her performance is **vital** to our theater company's success. (彼女の演技が我々の劇団の命運を握っている)

Notes : 語源はラテン語の "vita" (生命)。同じ語源を持つ単語に "vitamin" (ビタミン) があります。

---

107 mother tongue

[mʌ́ðer tʌ́ŋ]

Noun　Linguistics

Def : the first language that you learn from where you are a child

日 : 母語

Syn : native language

e. g. : What is your **mother tongue**? (あなたの母語は何ですか)

Notes : 音声学の授業で、「『舌』は『下』と混乱しないように『べろ』または『tongue (タン)』」を使います。みなさんが『おいしい、おいしい』と食べている牛タンの『タン』は『べろ』です」と言うと、必ず悲鳴が上がります。

---

108 pessimistic

[pèsəmístɪk]

Adjective　Basic

Def : thinking that bad things are more likely to happen than positive things

日 : 悲観的

Syn : hopeless, negative

e. g. : I feel **pessimistic** about us. I can't see how we have any future together. (私達の将来は悲観的だわ。一緒に未来を切り拓くことができるとは思えない)

Notes : If you want to talk about the future of anything (a project, a relationship, work), optimistic and **pessimistic** are two necessary words to express your feelings, whether positive or negative. 楽観的か悲観的か、気持ちを表すのにはこの2語ですね。

(一口アドバイス) 27　Be a "language detective"! Investigate new words and phrases.

109 narrator

[nəréɪtər]

Noun　Literature

Def : a person who tells a story

日 : 語り手

Syn : storyteller

e.g. : The first-person **narrator** tells the story with the first-person pronoun "I." （1 人称の語り手は「私」という 1 人称で話を語る）

Notes : 日本語の「ナレーター」とは発音が違います。小説における「視点」を語るときに必ず出てくる単語です。文学を学ぶ人は覚えましょう。

---

110 respectable

[rɪspéktəb(ə)l]

Adjective　Basic

Def : having a good reputation

日 : 立派な

Syn : good, honorable

e.g. : Kiyone comes from a **respectable** family. （清音は由緒ある家柄の出だ）

Notes : "respectable" は「上品ぶった」という皮肉なニュアンスを込めて使われるときもあります。"respectful"（礼儀正しい）と混同しないよう注意しましょう。"You should be respectful to your elders."（年長者には礼儀正しくしなさい）

---

111 promising

[prɑ́ːməsɪŋ]

Adjective　Conversation

Def : showing signs of potential future success

日 : 前途有望な

Syn : up-and-coming

e.g. : She is one of the most **promising** students in my class. （彼女は私のクラスで将来有望な学生の一人です）

Notes : 推薦書を書くとき "promising"（将来有望な）という言葉をよく使います。

---

112 ～-year-old

[jíər óuld]

Adjective　Basic

Def : having a particular age

日 : ～歳（の人）

Syn : NA

e.g. : She is teaching **six-year-old** children. （彼女は 6 歳児を教えている）

Notes : ハイフンで結んで形容詞にする際には、years と複数形にしないのがポイントです。また、a three-year-old car（登録から 3 年たった車）のように、（ハイフンでつなぐことによって）形容詞として使うことができるのです。

（一口アドバイス）28　会話をするには 2000 語必要です。

113 "Definitely!"

[défənətli]

Other　Conversation

Def : certainly

日 : もちろん、おっしゃる通り

Syn : absolutely

e.g. : "Do you want to come to the beach with us?" "**Definitely!**"（一緒に海に行きませんか？　もちろん行きますとも！）

Notes : My granddaughter, aged 9, used this expression frequently when she visited the U.S. そのまま使ってみましょう。

---

114 biased

[báɪəst]

Adjective　Academic

Def : showing favor to one side over another

日 : 偏った見方の

Syn : prejudiced, one-sided

e.g. : Older managers might be **biased** against younger workers. （年配の経営者は若年労働者に対して偏った見方をしているかもしれません）

Notes : This word is very commonly used in news stories about sports and politics. その報道は偏っている（Its reports are biased.）のように使われます。

---

115 vague

[véɪg]

Adjective　Academic

Def : unclear or uncertain

日 : あいまい、漠然

Syn : unclear, fuzzy

e.g. : I don't understand. Your ideas are a bit **vague**. （よくわからない。君の考えは少し曖昧だよ）

Notes : Important for academic writing and for discussing whether you understand something clearly or not. Generally, we want clear ideas and reasons, not vague ones. レポートで是非使ってみましょう。曖昧な答え（vague answer）もなるべく避けましょう。

---

116 indent

[ɪndént]

Verb　Academic

Def : begin the first line of a paragraph with some spaces

日 : インデント（字下げ）する

Syn : NA

e.g. : Please **indent** the paragraph. （段落の最初の語は引っ込めて書きなさい）

Notes : Remember that Japanese paragraphs get indented just one space, but in English it's 3-7 spaces. 動詞だけでなく indent は名詞でも使われますが、indentation という名詞形もあります。強勢の位置に気をつけましょう。

（一口アドバイス）29　If you don't run, you can't win. (Sybil, *Chariots of Fire*)

117 image

[ímɪdʒ]

Noun　Literature

Def : a mental picture

日 : イメージ、視覚的映像

Syn : picture, likeness

e.g. : The author uses the **image** of a rotten apple to show the society's degradation. (著者は腐ったリンゴのイメージを社会の堕落を表すために用いている)

Notes : 日本語で「イメージ」というと漠然とした印象を指す場合が多いですが、これは和製英語と考えてよいでしょう。英語では主に視覚的映像、心の中で再現された外部世界の一部を指します。詩的表現では、このイメージによって多面的な効果を生み出します。発音に注意しましょう。

---

118 verse

[vɔ́ːrs]

Noun　Literature

Def : words that are in the form of poetry

日 : 韻文、何番（歌などの）

Syn : poetry, stanza

e.g. : Do you know the author of the well-known **verses**? (その有名な詩の作者を知っていますか)

Notes : シェイクスピアは劇の中で "verse"（韻文）と "prose"（散文）を場面に合わせて見事に使い分けています。詩というと poem ですが、verse は詩の一部と考えられます。また歌の2番（a second verse）のように使うこともできます。

---

119 "Here you are."

[hˈɪər ju ˈɑːr]

Other　Conversation

Def : used when you are giving someone something

日 : はい、どうぞ。

Syn : "Here you go."

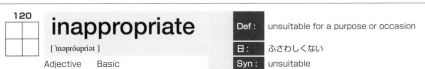

e.g. : "Please fill in that form. Need a pen? **Here you are.**" (その用紙に必要事項を書いてください。ペンいりますか？はい、どうぞ)

Notes : 単語だけを見ても、なぜこの意味になるかよくわかりませんが、日常的によく使う表現です。無言で何かを手渡すと無愛想で感じが悪いですね。この表現を覚えてすんなり使えるようにしておくと、相手に与える印象がずいぶん変わるはずです。

---

120 inappropriate

[ɪnəpróupriət]

Adjective　Basic

Def : unsuitable for a purpose or occasion

日 : ふさわしくない

Syn : unsuitable

e.g. : It is **inappropriate** to wear sunglasses in the classroom. (教室でサングラスをかけるのは不適切だ)

Notes : Knowing what is appropriate or inappropriate is important to function in society, whether it concerns manners, speech or clothing. 何が適切であるかは文化によっても異なりますね。

（一口アドバイス）30　A tower can only reach high, if it has a strong base. Master your fundamentals.

121 commodity

[kəmáːdəti]

Noun　Academic

Def : a product that can be traded, bought, or sold

日 : 商品

Syn : goods, wares

e. g. : Gold is a valuable **commodity**.
（金は高価な商品だ）

Notes : You will encounter this word when reading about/listening to news about financial markets. 経済ニュースでよく使われることばです。商品価格（commodity price）もあわせて覚えておきましょう。

122 agenda

[ədʒéndə]

Noun　Academic

Def : a list of things to be discussed at a meeting

日 : 議題

Syn : program

e. g. : I wrote the **agenda** of the next meeting in the last email. （最後のメールで次回の会議議題について書きました）

Notes : Used frequently when talking about business meetings. 会議ではなくてはならない単語です。

123 critical thinking

[krítɪk(ə)l θíŋkɪŋ]

Noun　Academic

Def : analytical thinking

日 : 論理的思考

Syn : NA

e. g. : Students are encouraged to develop **critical thinking** skills. （学生は批判的思考能力を身につける必要がある）

Notes : ここで言う「批判」は negative な意味はなく、logical とか rational な考え方を指す。

124 concrete

[kənkríːt]

Adjective　Basic

Def : based on real facts

日 : 具体的な

Syn : specific

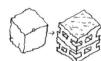

e. g. : We need more **concrete** ideas. Concrete details. （もっと具体案が欲しいな。具体的で詳細なものが）

Notes : Students need to express their ideas in concrete details, not vaguely. 本当ですね。"That's too vague. Can you be more concrete?" 強勢の位置に気をつけましょう。concrete の反対語は、abstract（抽象的な）です。

125 hook

[húk]

Noun　Academic

Def : a way of attracting attention

日 : つかみ

Syn : angle

e.g.: The **hook** in class is crucial to grab students' attention.（授業のはじめのつかみはとても重要だ）

Notes : プレゼンテーションや（模擬）授業で最も重要なのが、はじめの部分です。いかに聴衆（学生）に関心を持ってもらうかが勝負です。そのような「つかみ」にあたるのがこの単語です。フックですが、引っかけるという印象ですね。釣り竿についている「針」という意味でもあります。

---

126 ground rule (s)

[gráun(d)_rùːl]

Noun　Basic

Def : basic guidelines

日 : 基本原則

Syn : basic rule, principle

e.g.: No drink or food. This is the **ground rule** for using the computer room. Do you understand?（飲食禁止、これがコンピュータルーム使用の基本ルールです。分かりましたか）

Notes : Rules are rules.（規則は規則）という言い方があります。日本語でグラウンドルールと言われることも多くなってきました。野球用語では、特定の球場のみに適用されるルールという意味もあります。

---

127 masterpiece

[mǽstərpìːs]

Noun　Basic

Def : an excellent work of art such as a painting, film, or book

日 : 名作

Syn : great work, masterwork

e.g.: Many people say the statue of David is Michelangelo's **masterpiece**.（ダビデ像はミケランジェロの傑作だと多くの人は言う）

Notes : Great word for talking about art and culture. 芸術を語るには必須の単語ですね。駄作は total faliure, poor work などと呼ばれます。

---

128 at first

[ə(t)_fə́ːrst]

Adverb　Basic

Def : at the beginning

日 : 最初は

Syn : at the onset

e.g.: **At first**, almost none of the participants supported his idea.（最初は彼の考えは参加者のほとんどから賛同を得られなかった）

Notes : エッセイを見ていると、at first と first を混同しているものが案外多いです。First, ... Second, ... Finally ... と順序よく論理的に述べる際の transitions（つなぎ言葉）には at first ではなく First, Firstly を使い、at first はあくまでも最初「は」という意味で使いましょう。

（一口アドバイス）32　You're never wrong to do the right thing. (Ben, *The Intern*)

129 line(s)

[láɪn]

Noun　Literature

Def : the words an actor says

日 : セリフ

Syn : words of a role

e.g. : "To be or not to be" is a famous **line** from *Hamlet*. (「To be or not to be」は『ハムレット』に出てくる有名なセリフだ)

Notes : Notice the difference from the word "dialogue," which refers to all the lines in a film or work of fiction as a whole. だから、"Please learn your lines by next week." (あなたの台詞を…) ということになるのですね。

---

130 priority

[praɪɔ́ːrəti]

Noun　Conversation

Def : something that is very important and must be completed before other things

日 : 優先事項

Syn : first concern, preference

e.g. : Have you decided which matter has **priority**? (優先順位を決めましたか？)

Notes : 人生における、あなたの "priority" は何ですか？

---

131 impair

[ɪmpéər]

Verb　Conversation

Def : damage something, make it weaker, or prevent something functioning properly

日 : 弱める、損なう

Syn : hurt, damage

e.g. : His hearing was **impaired** by a high fever when he was a baby. (赤ちゃんの時の高熱で彼は耳を悪くした)

Notes : impair は良い関係を保つべきもの（友情、健康など）のバランスが崩れることを意味します (impair one's health, impair a good friendship など)。

---

132 culture

[kʌ́ltʃər]

Noun　Basic

Def : the habits, traditions, and beliefs of the people of a particular country, society, or group

日 : 文化

Syn : lifestyle, civilization

e.g. : Living in England, I've learned a lot about the **culture** of this country. (イングランドに住んで、その文化をじっくりと学んでいる)

Notes : 留学してみて感じるのは文化の違い。Brown (2014) によると Culture Shock には４段階あり、① Euphoria（幸福な時期 - 旅行などの短期滞在）② Culture Shock（ホームシック状態）③ Recovery（ショックからの立ち直り）④ Adaptation（異文化への順応）の経過をたどるとされます。あなたはどれを経験しましたか？

（一口アドバイス）33　Every day is a new day.

133 synonym

[sínənɪm]

Noun — Linguistics

Def: a word with the same or similar meaning as another

日: 同意語

Syn: NA

e.g.: "Love" and "affection" are **synonyms**. (love と affection は同義語だ)

Notes: "Syn-" means "same," and "-nym" means "name." ちなみに反意語は antonym です。antonym (No. 161) も参照して下さい。

---

134 current

[kʌ́rənt]

Adjective — Basic

Def: happening or existing now

日: 最新の

Syn: present, present-day

e.g.: You need to keep up with **current** events. (最近の出来事に疎くならないように気をつけなさい)

Notes: ニュースなどで最近の出来事、などというコーナーのタイトルとして登場します。何のことはないのですが、この言葉を聞いてピンと来るようにしておきたいですね。

---

135 sympathetic

[sìmpəθétɪk]

Adjective — Conversation

Def: feeling sorry for someone who is hurt or sad

日: 思いやりのある、好意的な

Syn: empathetic, supportive

e.g.: I don't think she is a very **sympathetic** person. (彼女は思いやりがある人だとは思えないね)

Notes: enthusiastic（情熱的）と一緒に覚えたい語です。反対語の antipathetic（反感をおぼえる）も一緒に覚えましょう。

---

136 tried to

[tráɪ(d)_tu]

Verb — Basic

Def: made an unsuccessful effort to do something

日: ～しようとした

Syn: attempted to, couldn't manage to

e.g.: He **tried to** bake a cake. (彼はケーキを焼こうとした [が失敗した])

Notes: In the past tense, "try to" always indicates a failed attempt. 現在形で使う場合にも、成功する可能性は低い意味合いで用いられます。

（一口アドバイス）34　数を当たれ、そのうち要領がわかる。

137 collocation

[kɑ̀ːləkéiʃən]

Noun Linguistics

Def : two or more words that occur together with a frequency greater than random probability would predict, e.g. "Merry Christmas".

日 : コロケーション（単語と単語のつながり）

Syn : NA

e. g. : The student asked, "What are the common **collocations** of this word?" (この単語のよく使われるコロケーションは何ですか？と学生が質問した)

Notes : Becoming aware of collocations helps you remember and use new vocabulary items naturally. 例えば、「意見を述べる」という場合、opinion のコロケーションとしては、give/express one's opinion と決まった動詞が使われることに注目しなければなりません。

138 verbal

[və́ːrb(ə)l]

Adjective Academic

Def : relating to spoken words

日 : 口頭の、言葉による

Syn : spoken, linguistic

e. g. : Yukina made a **verbal** promise to submit her assignment in the next session. （ゆきなは次の授業で課題を提出すると口約束をした）

Notes : 言語を介さないコミュニケーションが non-verbal communication であるように、verbal は言葉を用いたという意味になります。また、口頭でという意味も。口頭での説明は verbal explanation、書き言葉になると written（例えば、written notification、文書による通知）です。

139 fad

[fǽd]

Noun Conversation

Def : something that is popular for only a short period of time

日 : 一次的流行、気まぐれ

Syn : craze, fashion

e. g. : Tamagotchi? Yes, it's a **fad**! （たまごっち？それはブームですね）

Notes : fad は一時的な流行りもの。すぐにブームが去るものです。一方で trad は traditional の略語です。一時的な fashion (fad) と 長く留まる tradition (trad) の対比で意味がスッと理解できる瞬間を味わったのを覚えています。

140 in other words

[ɪn ˌʌðər wɔ́ːrdz]

Other Basic

Def : to say something using different words

日 : 言い換えれば

Syn : that is to say

e. g. : He gets angry when he can't have his own way. **In other words**, he's childish. （あの人は我を通すことができないとすぐ怒ります。すなわち、大人気ない）

Notes : A handy way to restate what you said and make it easy to understand. You can also use it to restate what someone else said and make sure you got it right. エッセイでは必須の表現ですね。

（一口アドバイス）35 Strong minds discuss ideas; average minds discuss events; weak minds discuss people.

141 dialogue

[dáɪələɔːɡ]

Noun   Communication

Def : conversation in a drama, story, etc

日 : 対話、やり取り

Syn : script

e.g. : Shiba Ryotaro is a master of **dialogue**. (司馬遼太郎の書いたダイアログが実に巧みです)

Notes : While translating *Ryoma ga yuku*, I thoroughly enjoyed the clever dialogue. It makes the characters come alive. 小説の会話の部分（セリフ）は情景を生き生きと映し出しますね。

142 accelerate

[əksélərèɪt]

Verb   Academic

Def : make something happen sooner or faster

日 : 加速する

Syn : go faster, speed up

e.g. : It's possible for our company to **accelerate** production half a month. (弊社がその生産を半月早めるのは可能だ)

Notes : This is an advanced level of vocabulary to use professionally or academically. 少し高度な英語です。accelerate growth であれば「成長を早める」という意味になります。

143 bold

[bóuld]

Adjective   Basic

Def : willing to take risks, brave

日 : 大胆な、勇敢な

Syn : brave, strong

e.g. : We need a **bold** idea. (大胆なアイデアがいるんです)

Notes : A simple and useful word. I think the concept is important too. I hope that our students will be bold in their lives and work. 力強く、大胆に！(Don't be so timid! Be confident! Be bold!) ちなみに色に関しては、a bold color（大胆な配色）になります。

144 questionnaire

[kwèstʃənéər]

Noun   Academic

Def : a set of questions about a certain subject

日 : 質問紙、アンケート

Syn : survey, research, inquiry

e.g. : Moe administered her **questionnaire** to 50 college students for her thesis. (モエは卒論の質問紙調査を50名の大学生に実施した)

Notes : アンケートはもう日本語になっている感もありますね。レストランなどでも「アンケートにお答えください」と紙が置いてあったりします。でも英語でアンケートといっても決して通じません。それはフランス語 (enquête) だから。気をつけましょう。Could you answer my questionnaire?

（一口アドバイス）36　話さないと話せません。

145 task

[tǽsk]

Noun　Basic

Def : a piece of work or activity that must be done

日 : 仕事

Syn : assignment, duty

e.g. : We will rely on your patience because this is a really difficult **task**. （あなたの辛抱強さを頼りにしているよ、これはとても難しい仕事なんでね）

Notes : 「仕事」といってもいろいろで、"task" の場合、誰かに課されたちょっとやっかいだけどとりあえずこなさなければならない仕事。作業部会（task force）に入った場合には、任務完了まで気を抜くことはできません。tusk になると（ゾウやセイウチの）牙です。

---

146 quit

[kwít]

Verb　Basic

Def : stop doing something

日 : やめる、中止する

Syn : give up, cease

e.g. : He **quit** the job. （彼はあっさり仕事をやめた）

Notes : 例文のように他動詞でも、He quit. と自動詞で使っても同じ意味になります。過去形の動詞変化は現在形と同じ quit です。stop と同じで、後ろには動名詞をとります。

---

147 creepy

[krí:pi]

Adjective　Conversation

Def : strange, odd, weird

日 : 不気味な、気持ちが悪い、いやらしい

Syn : obnoxious, weird

e.g. : "That old guy is staring at me! **Creepy!**" （あの人こちらをじっと見ているわ。気持ち悪い！）

Notes : Many young people use this word a lot. Seems useful. 例えば、"I don't like him. I think he is creepy." とか "That house has a creepy atmosphere." 不気味というのにピッタリです。使いすぎないように。

---

148 arrogant

[ǽrəgənt]

Adjective　Conversation

Def : believing that you are better than other people

日 : 傲慢な

Syn : cavalier, lofty, insolent

e.g. : She was still angry at his **arrogant** behavior at the party. （彼女はパーティでの彼の傲慢なふるまいにまだ腹を立てていた）

Notes : 留学中、"She is elegant." といったつもりなのに、発音が悪く、arrogant と聞き間違えられて、慌てたことがあります。

（一口アドバイス）37　Do not let what you cannot do interfere with what you can do. (John Wooden)

149

actually

[ǽktʃuəli]

Adverb　　Conversation

e.g.: His family seems to think Jun is a quiet, soft type of kid. **Actually**, he's noisy and a bully in school.（家族はジュンは静かで大人しい子だと思ってるみたい。でも学校ではやかましいし、いじめっ子なんだよ）

Def: used to indicate politeness when disagreeing with someone or saying no to a request

日: 実際には

Syn: in fact

Notes: This is a common way to express yourself in conversation. 日本人による誤用がとりわけ多い語のひとつ。辞書を引くと「実際に」という訳が出てきますが、そう考えて使うとだいたい誤用になります。かならず前に述べたこととは反対に思えるような、意外な情報を続けて述べなければなりません。それを知っていれば活用法の広い単語です。

150

"I don't mind."

[aɪ dõun(t)_máɪnd]

Other　　Conversation

e.g.: "**Do you mind** if I keep the door open? " "No, **I don't mind**." （ドアを開けっ放しでいいですか？かまいませんよ。）

Def: to be unconcerned about something

日: かまいません

Syn: It doesn't bother me. I don't care.

Notes: In Japanese nowadays some people say ドンマイ, but in English we don't say "Don't mind." We say either "I don't mind," or, when speaking to someone else, "Never mind." ドンマイには気をつけましょう。

151

optimistic

[àːptmístɪk]

Adjective　　Basic

e.g.: I am **optimistic** about our future. I think we can solve all our problems.（私達の未来は明るい。どんな問題でも解決できると思う）

Def: believing that something good will happen

日: 楽観的な

Syn: hopeful, positive

Notes: If you want to talk about the future of anything (a project, a relationship, work) optimistic and pessimistic are two necessary words to express your feelings, whether positive or negative. 楽観的か悲観的か、気持ちを表すのにはこの２語ですね。

152

flexible

[fléksəb(ə)l]

Adjective　　Basic

e.g.: Osamu is a **flexible** person and easy to get along with.（修は融通の利く人で付き合いやすい）

Def: able to adapt or change according to the situation

日: 柔軟な、融通がきく

Syn: not obstinate, easygoing, elastic

Notes: 「やわらか頭」という言い方が一昔前に流行したことを思い出します。

（一口アドバイス）38　Think like a queen. A queen is not afraid to fail. (Oprah Winfrey)

153 in one's shoes

[ɪn wənz ʃúːz]

Other　Conversation

Def : to try to see or understand things from someone else's perspective

日 : 〜の立場で

Syn : in one's place

e. g. : She's got everything: money, a gorgeous boyfriend, a nice house... What's it like **in her shoes**? (彼女、すべてを手に入れたわ、お金も、ハンサムな彼氏も、すてきな家も…。自分が彼女の立場だったらどんな感じかしら?)

Notes : 「〜の靴をはくと」ということですが、比喩的に、「もし(誰かと)同じ立場だったら」という仮定の状況を表します。実際はいてみたらサイズが合わなかったりして気持ち悪そうですが。

---

154 exhibition

[èksəbíʃən]

Noun　Basic

Def : an event at which things such as paintings or artifacts are displayed

日 : 展示

Syn : show, display, fair

e. g. : The international manga **exhibition** was held in Kyoto in 2016. (国際漫画展覧会が2016年に京都で開かれた)

Notes : 動詞の "exhibit" は [ɪgzíbɪt] と濁りますが、名詞の "exhibition" は [èksəbíʃən] と濁らないことに気をつけましょう。

---

155 italics

[ɪtǽlɪks]

Noun　Academic

Def : a style of writing or printing that slants diagonally to the right

日 : イタリック、斜体

Syn : NA

e. g. : Write titles of books and movies in **italics**. (本や映画のタイトルはイタリック体の活字で打とう)

Notes : Know the rules: quotation marks for titles of poems, songs, and chapters; italics for titles of books, magazines, newspapers, plays, movies, paintings, TV shows, and CD albums. Foreign words, stressed words, and internal dialogue also go in italics. イタリックのルールを覚えておきましょう。

---

156 enable

[ɪnéɪb(ə)l]

Verb　Basic

Def : facilitate someone or something

日 : …できるようにする

Syn : allow, empower

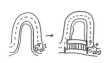

e. g. : Hope **enables** a person to take a step forward. (希望は人に一歩前に進むことを可能にする)

Notes : 中学3年生で、able, ability, enable と単語の派生形に興味をもつきっかけになったのが enable でした。

(一口アドバイス) 39　Family can never be judgmental. (Shashi, *English Vinglish*)

157 hymn

[hím]

Noun　Literature

Def : a religious song

日 : 賛美歌、聖歌

Syn : carol

e.g. : We sang **hymns** at his funeral.
（私たちは彼の葬儀で賛美歌を歌った）

Notes : "hymn" は「神を称える歌」、"anthem" は「国や英雄を称える歌」（"national anthem" は「国歌」）です。

---

158 terminal

[tə́ːrmən(ə)l]

Adjective　TOEIC

Def : relating to an end of something

日 : 終末の、終点の、終着駅の

Syn : final

e.g. : She was told by her doctor that her illness was **terminal**, but then she made a full recovery. （医者に末期と宣告されたが彼女は完全な回復を遂げた）

Notes : 終わりという意味でいろいろな状況で使われる単語です。例えば、空港ビルは terminal building と言われますし、病気だと、末期（fatal, mortal）という意味になります。

---

159 consume

[kəns(j)úːm]

Verb　Basic

Def : eat, drink or use something

日 : 食べる・飲む、消費する

Syn : eat up, use up

e.g. : As a nation, we **consume** a huge amount of fish. （国レベルでは莫大な魚を消費している）

Notes : A useful word to know, especially in its noun form: consumption. そうそう消費税は consumption tax ですね。

---

160 attire

[ətáɪər]

Noun　Basic

Def : clothes, especially for a special or formal occasion

日 : 盛装

Syn : dress, clothing

e.g. : Audrey Hepburn appeared on the stage in the **attire** of a princess. （オードリー・ヘップバーンは王女の扮装で舞台に登場した）

Notes : "attire" は「服装」を表す少しフォーマルな表現です。

（一口アドバイス）40　You constantly change. Change for the better.

161 antonym

[ǽntənìm]

Noun　Linguistics

Def : a word that has opposite meaning to another word

日 : 反意語

Syn : opposite

e.g. : "Give" and "take" are **antonyms**. (Give と Take は反意語の関係だ)

Notes : "Ant-" means "opposite," and "-nym" means "name." 接頭辞の ant は反対の、nym は名前を表します。Synonym は同意語という意味になります。"syn" は "same" という意味ですね。Synonym (No. 133) も参照して下さい。

162 thesis statement

[θíːsɪ(s)_stéɪtmənt]

Noun　Academic

Def : the sentence that states the main idea of a writing assignment and helps control the ideas within the paper

日 : 主題文

Syn : NA

e.g. : A strong **thesis statement** helps you to organize an essay clearly. (主題文があると全体の構成が明確になる)

Notes : A basic thesis statement might begin: "This essay will…" A more advanced thesis statement makes a claim and states the contents of the claim, e.g. "There are three reasons why…" 構成と密接に関連しますね。

163 naive

[nɑɪ́ːv]

Adjective　Basic

Def : showing a lack of experience, wisdom, or judgment

日 : 世間知らずな

Syn : innocent, inexperienced, green

e.g. : We should not look to her for leadership, because she is **naive** and childish. (彼女は世間知らずで幼稚だからリーダーを任せることはできない)

Notes : 日本語で「ナイーブ」というと繊細な良いイメージがありますが、英語では「世間知らず」の意味です。使い方に注意しましょう。

164 brochure

[brouʃúər]

Noun　TOEIC

Def : a short printed publication

日 : パンフレット

Syn : pamphlet, booklet, flyer

e.g. : The new **brochures** were printed yesterday. (昨日、新しいパンフレットが印刷された)

Notes : The word "brochure," which originates from French, is used more frequently than "pamphlet." 発音にも気をつけましょう。強勢は後ろの音節につきます。

（一口アドバイス）41　生きるんだ、そう決意したんだから。 (Drabble, *Jerusalem the Golden*)

165

monologue

[mάːnəlɔ̀ːg]

Noun　Communication

Def : a long speech

日 : 独白

Syn : talk, speech

e.g. : The comedian's opening **monologue** was hilarious. （冒頭の独白は素晴らしかった）

Notes : Late-night TV shows in the U.S. begin with a comic monologue based on events in the news. One of my favorites is Stephen Colbert's *The Late Show*. 英語学習にも適した教材ですね。

166

obese

[oubíːs]

Adjective　Basic

Def : having a Body Mass Index (BMI) of more than 30, overweight

日 : 肥満の

Syn : fat, fleshy

e.g. : Heavy people are not necessarily **obese**. （体重が重いからといって、必ずしも肥満とは限らない）

Notes : obese は医学用語。健康を損なうような太り方をしている場合に使われます。名詞形は "obesity"（肥満）で、ニュースなどによく登場します。

167

available

[əvéɪləb(ə)l]

Adjective　Conversation

Def : not busy, free

日 : 空いている、時間がある

Syn : accessible

e.g. : "Professor Kodama, will you be **available** tomorrow 2 pm? I have a question about the lecture last week." （児玉先生、明日の午後 2 時にお時間いただけますか。先週の講義について質問があるのですが）

Notes : Are you available today? と言われて「私は物じゃないんだけど」なんて思わないように。この語は人にも使えます。先生とアポイントメントを取るときに使いましょう。Can I ask you a favor?（御願いがあるのですが）で話し始め、この例文を使うといいでしょう。

168

prefix

[príːfɪks]

Noun　Linguistics

Def : a word part that is added to the beginning of a word, e.g. "un-," or "dis-."

日 : 接頭辞

Syn : NA

e.g. : Knowing the meanings of **prefixes** can help you understand the meanings of new words. （接頭辞を知っていると新しい単語の意味を理解しやすくなります）

Notes : For example, "un-" is a prefix that means "not," so "unhappy" means "not happy." ちなみに接尾辞は suffix です。

（一口アドバイス）42　We do these things not to change the world, but so that the world will not change us. (Mahatma Gandhi)

169

endure

[ɪnd(j)úər]

Verb　　Basic

Def :	patiently experience something difficult or unpleasant
日 :	我慢する、耐える
Syn :	put up with, abide

e. g. : I can't **endure** your rudeness anymore!（君の無礼には我慢がならん）

Notes : In all our lives we have to endure people or situations we don't like, or maybe we feel we cannot endure things any more . For Japanese people the word 我慢 is important. So, "endurance" and "endure" are important words to know in English too. ああもう我慢できない（I can't endure it. Please stop.）なんて。

170

thrive

[θráɪv]

Verb　　Basic

Def :	grow, develop, or be successful
日 :	繁栄する
Syn :	flourish, prosper

e. g. : Children can **thrive** even in difficult circumstances if they are given proper support.（過酷な状況でも、ちゃんとした支援があれば、子供たちは元気に育つ）

Notes : "survive" は「死なずに生き延びること」、"thrive" は「繁栄していくこと」。人間は単に生き延びるのではなく繁栄してゆかねばならぬ（Humans should thrive not just survive.）。京都は観光で繁栄する（Kyoto thrives on tourism.）というようにも使われます。

171

asset

[æset]

Noun　　Academic

Def :	something valuable that belongs to a person or organization
日 :	資産、財産
Syn :	treasure

e. g. : I know that Mai will be a great **asset** to your university.（マイがあなたの大学の貴重な財産になることは間違いありません）

Notes : 例文のように推薦状のしめくくりでもよく使われることばです。treasure だけでなくこのような類似の別の言葉を使うことによって豊かな文章表現になります。

172

sign language

[sáɪn læ̀ŋgwɪdʒ]

Noun　　Communication

Def :	a language that uses hand gestures to communicate
日 :	手話
Syn :	NA

e. g. : The two deaf people were using **sign language** to communicate.（耳の不自由な二人が手話を使ってコミュニケーションしていた）

Notes : When I ask students for examples of non-verbal communication (that is, communication without words), one of the examples they give is always sign language. However, in fact, sign language does use words. We can say that sign language is verbal (that is, it uses words) but not vocal (that is, it does not use the sound of the voice). 手話は言語であってノンバーバルコミュニケーションではないのですね。

（一口アドバイス）43　Do whatever you want and money follows.

173

challenge

[tʃǽlɪndʒ]

Verb　Basic

Def : attack, dare or show disagreement with something

日 : 異議を唱える

Syn : question, doubt, protest

e.g. : By refusing to participate in the class, she **challenged** the teacher's authority. (授業に参加しないことにより、彼女は教師の権威に意義を唱えた)

Notes : "Challenge" does not mean "try." チャレンジ = 挑戦すると思ってしまいますが、動詞として使うと「意義を唱えたり」、「疑う」という意味です。また、She challenged him to a game of billiards. (彼女はビリヤードのゲームを挑んできた) という意味もあります。形容詞で challenging になると「やりがいがあるが困難を伴う厳しいもの」というニュアンスがあることに注意しましょう。名詞では日本語と同じ意味です。

174

brand

[brǽnd]

Noun　Basic

Def : the name and image of a type of product

日 : 銘柄

Syn : trademark

e.g. : What **brand** of black tea do you usually drink? (いつもどの銘柄の紅茶を飲んでいますか)

Notes : いわゆるブランドものという際に、つい "a brand bag" というような言い方をしてしまいそうになりますが、実際には、"a designer pen (cup)" (ブランドもののペン、カップ) と表現します。「マリエは大金を払ってブランドのカバンを購入した」であれば、Marie spent a lot of money on a designer bag. です。brand は銘柄という意味で、高級品という意味はありません。

175

part of speech

[pɑ́ːrt‿əv spíːtʃ]

Noun　Linguistics

Def : a class of words based on function, such as noun, verb, adjective, etc.

日 : 品詞

Syn : word class

e.g. : What **part of speech** is that word? Is it an adverb or an adjective? (その単語の品詞は何でしょうか。副詞ですか、それとも形容詞?)

Notes : Words change their shape as they become different parts of speech; it is very useful to be able to identify them. 品詞についての知識も大切ですね。前置詞 (preposition) や接続詞 (conjunction) のような語も、英語で言えるようにしておきましょう。

176

lick

[lík]

Verb　Basic

Def : touch with the tongue

日 : なめる

Syn : lap, taste

e.g. : The girl **lick**ed her ice cream cone. (少女はアイスクリームをなめていた)

Notes : 特に犬好きの人またはアイスクリームが好きな人は知っておかなければならない単語です。

(一口アドバイス) 44　Education is what survives when what has been learned has been forgotten. (B. F. Skinner)

177 happen to know

[hǽpən tu nóu]

Verb　　Conversation

Def : a polite way of asking someone if they know something

日 : （ひょっとして）〜をご存じですか？

Syn : know

e. g. : Do you **happen to know** where a good ramen restaurant is? (どこかおいしいラーメン屋さん、ご存じですか)

Notes : 丁寧に言う場面で使ってみましょう。

---

178 headquarters

[hédkwɔ̀ːrtərz]

Noun　　TOEIC

Def : the place from which a leader runs an organisation

日 : 本社（HQ）

Syn : main/head office, home

e. g. : They had to contact **headquarters** about the big problem. (大きな問題については本部まで連絡しなければならなかった)

Notes : ビジネスやアクション映画でよく使われますね。A good word to know. 通常複数形で使われます。

---

179 "That's awful."

[ðǽts_ɔ́ːf(ə)l]

Other　　Conversation

Def : an expression of sympathy

日 : 大変

Syn : "That's terrible/dreadful."

e. g. : "Your bike was stolen? **That's awful!**" (自転車が盗まれたって？それはひどい)

Notes : Useful to express sympathy. Some students only seem to know "Oh no!" and "Oh my God!" This is better. 同情を表す際に使ってみましょう。

---

180 indigenous

[ɪndídʒənəs]

Adjective　　Culture

Def : belonging to a particular place by birth or origin

日 : 先住の、土着の

Syn : native

e. g. : The Ainu are **indigenous** people of Japan, and the original meaning of "Ainu" is human. (アイヌ民族は日本の先住民であり、アイヌとはもともと「人間」という意味である)

Notes : 同じ意味で native という語がありますが、大学レベルでは indigenous が必須です。先住民は indigenous people、その言語は indigenous language です。

（一口アドバイス）45　Play word games, like crossword puzzles.

181 transmit

[trænsmít]

Verb　TOEIC

Def: send from one person or place to another

日: 伝達する

Syn: transfer, convey

e.g.: I will **transmit** the information to the world. （私はその情報を世界に発信する）

Notes: This is a word frequently used in tele-communications. インターネットやテレビの情報発信 (transmit information) によく使われますね。また、ウイルス感染 (transmit the virus) のような場合にも用いられます。

---

182 congratulations

[kəŋgrætʃəléɪʃənz]

Noun　Basic

Def: words expressing praise or good wishes

日: 祝辞

Syn: compliments

e.g.: We sent them **congratulations** and good wishes for a long and happy life together. （私たちは彼らに祝辞を送り、末永い幸せを願った）

Notes: 複数形にするのを忘れないように。「おめでとう！」は "Congratulations!" です。

---

183 negotiate

[nəgóuʃìeɪt]

Verb　TOEIC

Def: try to reach an agreement or compromise by discussion with others

日: 交渉する、話し合って取り決める

Syn: consult, arrange

e.g.: We need to **negotiate** with the director right now. （今すぐ演出家と話し合う必要がある）

Notes: シェイクスピアの『十二夜』（Twelfth Night）の中で、オリヴィアが彼女の美しさをほめたたえるヴァイオラに向かって言う台詞 "Have you any commission from your lord to negotiate with my face?" （あなたはご主人から私の顔と交渉するよう言いつかってきたの？）が印象に残っています。

---

184 anxiety

[æŋzáɪəti]

Noun　Basic

Def: a feeling of worry about something in the future

日: 不安

Syn: uneasiness, nervousness

e.g.: Many learners of a foreign language suffer from language learning **anxiety** in the classroom. （外国語学習者の多くは教室で不安にかられることが多い）

Notes: There are many academics around the world who are researching the various reasons why language learners experience anxiety in the classroom and how their feelings of anxiety are related to their motivation. 形容詞形では anxious about〜（…に不安を感じる）、anxious to〜（…したい）と意味がわかれます。

（一口アドバイス）46　Set goals. Reach them. Feel good. Set new goals.

185

do the dishes

[dú: ðə díʃɪz]

Other　Conversation

Def : wash dishes

日 : 皿洗いをする

Syn : wash up

e.g. : "I'll do the laundry, so will you **do the dishes**?"（洗濯は私がやるから、あなたは皿洗いをしてよ）

Notes : 「皿を洗う」となると、どうしても "wash" という動詞が頭に浮かぶかもしれません。"wash" だと「洗う」という具体的な動きが連想されるので、家事としての皿洗いをするというときは "do the dishes" が自然です。定冠詞 "the" も忘れずに。

186

illiterate

[ɪlítərət]

Adjective　Conversation

Def : unable to read or write

日 : 無知な、読み書きができない

Syn : uneducated, ignorant

e.g. : I am computer **illiterate**.（コンピューターのことは何も知らない）

Notes : literature（文学）の形容詞が literate で「教養のある」という意味だと知ったとき、当たり前のことですが、教養はやはり書物から得るものなのだと思いました。教養のある（literate）を使って、"She is computer literate."（彼女はコンピューターを使える）のように表現することもできます。

187

rhyme

[ráɪm]

Noun　Literature

Def : a word that has the same sound as another, e.g. "time" and "line"

日 : 韻

Syn : tune, rhythm

e.g. : Some poems have the pattern of **rhymes** at the end of each line.（行末ごとに韻を踏む形態の詩がある）

Notes : 英語の詩は（伝統的に）韻を踏むので、短い詩を "rhyme" ということもあります。マザーグースもイギリスでは "nursery rhymes" と呼びます。

188

soul

[sóul]

Noun　Basic

Def : the spiritual part of a person; a person

日 : 魂、人間

Syn : spirit, person

e.g. : Don't tell a **soul** that we met.（私たちが会ったことは他言しないでください）

Notes : "soul" は本来 "body"（肉体）に対する「魂」の意味ですが、転じて「人間」を指します。"body and soul" は「身も心も、全身全霊」という意味になります。

（一口アドバイス）47　Use the words you have learned.

189 sensitive

[sénsətɪv]

Adjective　Basic

Def : easily affected

日 : 敏感な、繊細な

Syn : delicate, acute

e.g. : Spring is a nasty season for those who are **sensitive** to pollen. (春は花粉に敏感な人にとっては嫌な季節だ)

Notes : 英語で「繊細な」は "naive" ではなく "sensitive" または "delicate" を用います。例えば、私の目は光に弱いという場合には、My eyes are sensitive to light と表現します。「分別のある」（sensible）と区別して覚えましょう。

190 addiction

[ədíkʃən]

Noun　Academic

Def : the condition of being unable to stop doing something that is harmful to you

日 : 中毒、ふけること

Syn : dependence, obsession, attachment

e.g. : He conquered drug **addiction**. (彼は薬物中毒を克服した)

Notes : He had an addiction to alcohol (drug, videogames). などと中毒状況を説明するのになくてはならない単語です。すべてにおいて "addict"（動詞）しすぎることはよくない。

191 stanza

[stǽnzə]

Noun　Literature

Def : a group of lines of poetry forming a unit

日 : 節、連（詩の一区切り）

Syn : verse

e.g. : This poem has 7 **stanzas** of 4 lines. (この詩には 4 行の連が 7 つある)

Notes : 詩を語る場合の基本単語です。歌の 1 番、2 番という際には、verse を用います。

192 debt

[dét]

Noun　Conversation

Def : an amount of money that you owe someone

日 : 借金、借り

Syn : financial obligation, liabilities

e.g. : I worked hard after college to repay my **debts**. (借金を返済するために大学卒業後一生懸命働いた)

Notes : Remember, the "b" in this word is silent! 発音に要注意です。最近よく見かける debit card の debit には借金という意味がありますが、お金を銀行から引き落とすという意味で使われています。

（一口アドバイス）48　ありのままなんてない、無理して、やや我慢してがんばらなくては。（宮崎駿）

193

concentration

[kὰːnsəntréɪʃən]

Noun　Basic

Def : the ability to focus on a single thing

日 : 集中力

Syn : attention, absorption

e.g.: The noise disturbed her **concentration.**（騒音で彼女の集中力は乱れた）

Notes : TOEIC や TOEFL の受験で、英語力の次に大切なのが concentration ですね。ちなみにトランプ（cards）の神経衰弱は英語では concentration といいます。集中度が勝負なだけに分かる気がしますね。

194

latest

[léɪtɪst]

Adjective　Basic

Def : newest or most recent

日 : 最近の、最新の

Syn : newest, current

e.g.: Have you read Haruki Murakami's **latest** novel?（村上春樹の最新作を読みましたか？）

Notes : 一番最後に来るものが、一番新しいものになる、ということですね。

195

irony

[áɪrəni]

Noun　Literature

Def : the use of words that are the opposite of what you mean to say

日 : 皮肉、あてこすり

Syn : ridicule, satire

e.g.: This novel is filled with **irony.**（この小説はたくさんの皮肉に満ちている）

Notes : 皮肉とは、実際とは反対のことを述べる表現です。例えば、粗末な食事に対して、「えらいご馳走ですね」と言うことです。

196

plastic

[plǽstɪk]

Noun　Current

Def : credit cards or other types of plastic cards that can be used to pay for things

日 : クレジットカード

Syn : credit cards

e.g.: Today people are used to paying with **plastic.**（クレジットカードで支払いするのが当たり前になってきた）

Notes : この plastic は曲者です。クレジットカード以外にも買い物の際に、Paper or plastic?（袋は紙にしますか、ビニール袋にされますか）と聞かれることがあり、私達はどうもプラスチックというとすごい袋を期待するのですが、大抵ペラペラのビニール袋です。また、plastic surgery で「美容整形外科」という意味になります。

（一口アドバイス）49　There is a budding morrow in midnight. (Christina Rossetti)

197

"Happy New Year!"

[hǽpi n(j)úː jíər]

Phrase　Conversation

Def : greetings on New Year's Day

日 : 新年おめでとう

Syn : Greetings for the new year.

e.g. : Happy New Year! （新年あけましておめでとうございます）

Notes : "A Happy New Year!" とどちらを使うべきかと年賀状を見る度に思いませんか？日本の年賀状システムでは "Happy New Year!" が正解です。もっとも事前に届くようなグリーティングカードには "I wish you a merry Christmas and a happy New Year!" と書きます。"Happy (Birthday, Easter, Valentine, Halloween, Holiday Season) !" なども同様です。覚えて使ってみましょう。

198

dismiss

[dɪsmís]

Verb　Academic

Def : allow someone to leave, decide that something is not worthy of consideration

日 : 却下する

Syn : reject, expel, release

e.g. : Maryland judge **dismissed** Donald's suit against his wife. （メリーランド州の裁判官は、妻に対するドナルドの訴えを却下した）

Notes : dismiss には 解散させる の意味も有り、"Class is dismissed." は、先生が授業の終わりを告げる決まり文句です。

199

come to this

[kʌ́m tu ðís]

Verb　Literature

Def : result in this situation

日 : 結局こうなる

Syn : end up

e.g. : Since it has **come to this**, we had no choice but to cooperate with Mari. （こうなった以上はマリに協力するしか手はなかった）

Notes : 小説ではよく出てくる表現です。「こうなるとは思ってもみなかった」(I never thought it would come to this.) のように。

200

exaggerate

[ɪgzǽdʒərèɪt]

Verb　Academic

Def : say something is larger, better, or worse than it really is

日 : 大げさに言う（考える）

Syn : overdo, overstate, magnify

e.g. : "Don't **exaggerate**. Tell the truth." （誇張しないで真実を述べなさい）

Notes : The adjective "exaggerated" is also useful to describe people's expressions or to talk about the arts, especially performing arts. 例えば、"I don't like that actor. His acting is so exaggerated!" （大げさすぎる）なんていうこともできますね。

（一口アドバイス）50　Challenge the status quo. (Simon Sinek)

Part 3

Transition

"When I was five years old, my mother always told me

that happiness was the key to life.

When I went to school, they asked me what I wanted to be when I grew up. I wrote

down 'happy'. They told me I didn't understand the assignment, and I told them

they didn't understand life."

(John Lennon)

Note: Attributed to John Lennon, but without confirmed evidence.

201 authentic

[ɔ:θéntɪk]

Adjective　Conversation

Def : real and not fake

日 : 本物の

Syn : real, genuine, true

e.g.: I'd like to practice my English in an **authentic** situation. (英語を本場の状況で練習したい)

Notes : リスニング練習の目的は、実生活の中で聞こえてくる authentic language sound から情報を聴きとり理解することにあります。authentic な英語は決して（リスニングの課題のように）聴きとりやすいものばかりではないですが英語力向上に必要です。

---

202 make a difference

[mêɪk_ə dífərəns]

Verb　Basic

Def : have a noticeable positive effect

日 : 効果がある

Syn : affect, count

e.g.: That teacher really **made a difference** in the lives of her students. (あの教師は生徒たちに本当にすばらしい影響を与えました)

Notes : Extremely useful. Applies to big things or small. e.g. I added sugar to the spaghetti sauce and it really made a difference! (スパゲッティ・ソースに砂糖を加えてみたら、ずっと美味しくなりました) スピーチでもよく使われるイディオムです。

---

203 party pooper

[pɑ́ːti pùːpər]

Noun　Current

Def : someone who spoils others' fun

日 : （楽しい）空気を壊す人、盛り上がらない人

Syn : killjoy, wet blanket

e.g.: "Don't be such a **party pooper**. Come join the fun!" (Party pooper [盛り上がらない人]) になるな。みんなと一緒に楽しもうよ)

Notes : A gently teasing expression used among friends. これはまじめに考えすぎずに、気楽に使える、面白い表現です。

---

204 diversity

[daɪvə́ːrsəti]

Noun　Culture

Def : having various people with different cultures, ethnicities, social backgrounds, physical and mental abilities

日 : 多様性

Syn : heterogeneity, variety

e.g.: Vancouver, BC, Canada is known for its cultural **diversity**. (カナダのバンクーバーはその文化の多様性で有名だ)

Notes : In this age of globalization, we see more diversity in our schools, the workplace, and in our individual societies all around us. 多様性は重要なカギですね。

（一口アドバイス）51　Seize the day. (Mr. Keating, *The Dead Poets Society*)

205 lessen

[lés(ə)n]

Verb　Basic

Def : become or make something smaller

日 : 減らす

Syn : reduce

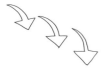

e.g. : Learners continue to be exposed to English to **lessen** the influence of their mother tongue. (母語の影響を減らすためには継続的に英語に触れておく必要がある)

Notes : lesson に似た単語ですが、スペルは lessen で、decrease の類似語です。

---

206 immutable

[ɪmjúːtəb(ə)l]

Adjective　Literature

Def : never changing, or unable to be changed

日 : 変わらない

Syn : unchanging

e.g. : In comparison with cities, Weatherbury was **immutable**. (都会と比べると、ウェザーベリーは不変であった) (Hardy, 1874)

Notes : これは難しい単語ですが、覚えましょう。反意語は mutable（変化する）です。例えば、Language is mutable（言語は変化する）のように使われます。Thomas Hardy（1840-1928）の初期の傑作小説 *Far from the Madding Crowd*（1874）の中から、少し難しい単語を拾ってみました。特に文学好きの卒業生のために。以下（Hardy, 1874）と記載したものはこの出典です。

---

207 public relations (PR)

[pʌ́blɪ(k)_rɪléɪʃənz]

Noun　TOEIC

Def : the activity of maintaining an organization's positive public image

日 : 広報

Syn : social relations

e.g. : Toru belongs to the **public relations** office. (徹は広報室に所属している)

Notes : Good to know this word in the communications or marketing industry. TOEIC 用の語彙ですが、PR というのは日本語でもよく使いますね。

---

208 rudimentary

[rùːdəméntəri]

Adjective　Academic

Def : basic, not complex

日 : 初歩的な

Syn : basic

e.g. : To improve English skills, **rudimentary** elements of English such as grammar or basic vocabulary are indispensable. (英語を上達させるには、基礎的な文法や語彙は不可欠だ)

Notes : 「初歩的な」の少し難しい言い方。辞書をみると「正式」と表示してあるのは、academic situation で使う用語という意味です。大学生の英語を学んでいる気持ちになる語彙です。

（一口アドバイス）52　Everything happens for the best.

209

seduce

[sɪd(j)úːs]

Verb   TOEIC

Def : trick someone into doing something by making it seem attractive

日 : 誘惑する

Syn : attract

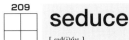

e.g. : Advertisements in magazines and on television are cleverly created to **seduce** young people into buying things they don't need. (雑誌やテレビの広告は、いらないものを買わせるよう、若い人々を誘惑するよう巧みに作られている)

Notes : 外国の街中を歩いているとよく、seduce という看板を見かけます。大抵怪しい店ですが、chocolate seduction（チョコレートの誘惑）や seduction of power（権力の誘惑）のように使うこともできます。

210

milieu

[miːljə́ː]

Noun   TOEIC

Def : (social) environment

日 : 環境、境遇

Syn : surroundings

e.g. : We need to pay attention to the social **milieu** of the period when Joseph Hardy Neesima founded Doshisha. (新島襄が同志社を創立した時代の社会環境を考慮する必要がある)

Notes : milieu は元々フランス語で「中心」という意味です。そこから中心にいる人間を取り囲む周囲の状態を意味するようになりました。social milieu（社会環境）として覚えておきましょう。語の後半に強勢が置かれます。

211

indispensable

[ˌɪndɪspénsəb(ə)l]

Adjective   Basic

Def : very important; necessary

日 : 不可欠な

Syn : necessary

e.g. : On a camping trip, a flashlight is **indispensable**. (キャンプに懐中電灯は不可欠だ)

Notes : Years ago I looked up many words that I wanted to know in Japanese. This was one. It is a more adult and sophisticated alternative to the word, necessary. 例えば、"You are indispensable to the success of this project." なんていわれると嬉しいですね。

212

epitome

[ɪpítəmi]

Noun   Literature

Def : a perfect example

日 : 典型、縮図

Syn : representation, embodiment

e.g. : Mother Teresa was an **epitome** of love and hope. (マザー・テレサ は愛と希望そのものでした)

Notes : epitome は representation（表象）の意味ですが、こういう表現ができると洗練された感じがします。an advanced level of vocabulary です。

（一口アドバイス）53　真理は平凡なり、平凡なる真理に透徹せよ。

213 irrelevant

[ɪrélǝvǝnt]

Adjective　Basic

Def : unrelated to the issue being discussed; off the subject

日 : 関係ない

Syn : unrelated, unimportant

e. g. : I'm sorry, but that point is **irrelevant.** （それは関係ないですよ）

Notes : Useful for conversation and also academic writing. 会話でもライティングでも使えますね。

---

214 all or nothing

[ɔ́:l ǝr nʌ́θɪŋ]

Other　Communication

Def : doing something either completely or not at all

日 : 完全解答

Syn : NA

e. g. : Jim could not bear it unless he was the top of the class. It was **all or nothing** with him. （ジムはクラスで一番でなければ嫌だった。彼にとっては一番でなければ意味がないのであった）

Notes : 高校の生物で「全か無かの法則」を習いました。英語では、all-or-nothing（又は all-or-none）law と表されます。全か無か、完全解答、イエスかノーか、いちかばちか、中途半端は駄目…という場面もありますね。

---

215 eclipse

[ɪklíps]

Noun　Basic

Def : when the sun is covered by the moon, or the moon is covered by the earth's shadow

日 : 月食、日食

Syn : NA

e. g. : I witnessed a total solar **eclipse** yesterday. （昨日、皆既日食を見た）

Notes : 月食は a lunar eclipse です。This word can also be used as a verb meaning "outshine": Though she was a talented writer, she was eclipsed by her sister.

---

216 imitate

[ímǝtèɪt]

Verb　Basic

Def : copy someone's voice or action

日 : まねする

Syn : mimic, copy

e. g. : He made us laugh by **imitating** our teacher perfectly. （彼は先生の完璧なまねをしてみんなを笑わせた）

Notes : Imitating is a universal human impulse. It can be funny and it is also a fundamental way of learning a language. 確かに、こどもは親のまねをしますね（Children usually imitate their parents.）。

（一口アドバイス）54　There is no life without some pressure. (Declan Donnellan)

217 ubiquitous

[ju(:)bíkwətəs]

Adjective Conversation

e.g.: Police boxes are **ubiquitous** in Japan. (日本では交番がどこにでもある)

Def: found everywhere

日: どこにでもある

Syn: common, everywhere

Notes: This is much more interesting and emphatic than saying something is "common." Some things that are ubiquitous in Japan puzzle me: why, for example, does everyone make the "V" sign when having their picture taken? This is definitely not ubiquitous in other countries. common の代わりにこの単語を使ってみたいですね。

---

218 on the house

[ɑn ðə háus]

Other Conversation

e.g.: No need to pay. Coffee refills are **on the house**. (お代はいりませんよ。コーヒーのお代わりは店のおごりです)

Def: given to you free by a business

日: 店からのおごりで

Syn: free, free of charge

Notes: Many students think that サービス in Japanese can just be changed to "service" in English, but it cannot. 日本語と英語でサービスの意味が異なります。有名なものに Morning service があります。英語では「教会の朝のお祈り」という意味です。

---

219 impact

[ímpækt]

Noun Conversation

e.g.: The experience made a huge **impact** on the girl. (その経験は少女に大きな影響を与えた)

Def: a significant influence or effect on something

日: 影響、衝撃

Syn: influence

Notes: カタカナ発音でも安心して使える語の一つです。映画の題名にも Deep Impact (1998) があります。

---

220 narrative

[nérətɪv]

Noun Academic

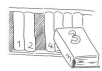

e.g.: When you read a **narrative**, imagine the situation where the story is told. (物語を読むのならその情景を思い浮かべて読みなさい)

Def: a story or a description of a series of events

日: 物語

Syn: story

Notes: 読みものは、小説などの物語 (narrative) と新聞や論文のような説明文 (expository writing) に大きく分類することができます。

（一口アドバイス）55　時には寄り道してみましょう。

contemporary

[kəntémpərèri]

Adjective　　Basic

Def : existing or happening now or at the same time

日 : （～と）同時代の、現代の

Syn : modern, current

e. g. : William Shakespeare was **contemporary** with Cervantes. （シェイクスピアはセルバンテスと同時代に生きていた）

Notes : *Shakespeare Our Contemporary* （『シェイクスピアはわれらの同時代人』ヤン・コット著、1974年）という本もあります。またこの題名のように名詞（同時期の人）として使うこともできます。

---

instinctively

[ɪnstíŋ(k)tɪvli]

Adverb　　Literature

Def : naturally and without thinking, automatic

日 : 本能的に

Syn : intuitively

e. g. : Diana was the goddess whom Bathsheba **instinctively** adored. （ダイアナ神は、バスシバが本能的に崇拝した女神であった）（Hardy, 1874）

Notes : この単語は難しくないですが、いろいろな場面で使われます。本能（instinct）、本能に頼る（rely on instinct）など。Steven Pinker が 1994 年に出版した本の題名は *The Language Instinct* （『本能としての言語』）でした。

---

valid

[vǽlɪd]

Adjective　　Academic

Def : based on accepted truth or reason

日 : 妥当（適切）な、有効な

Syn : reasonable

2017/09/26

Credit
XXXX-XXXX
2021/12

e. g. : Mai, you need to have a **valid** research instrument for your graduation thesis. （まいさん、卒論には妥当な研究手法が必要ですよ）

Notes : 卒業研究で調査によく使う方法に質問紙法（Questionnaire）があります。そこで重要になるのが「妥当性（validity）」。つまり、調査内容が質問紙に含まれているかどうか。信頼性（reliability）とともに卒業論文には不可欠の要素です（作成には時間がかかります）。

---

sophisticated

[səfístɪkèɪtəd]

Adjective　　Basic

Def : highly complex, experienced or knowledgeable.

日 : 洗練された、高い教養のある

Syn : refined, cultivated

e. g. : *Kaiseki* is the most **sophisticated** Japanese cuisine. （懐石料理は最も洗練された日本料理である）

Notes : We all need some simple pleasures but we all need sophisticated culture too. It lifts us up. The opposite of sophisticated may be "vulgar." I remember a student once said to me, "I want to be a sophisticated person, never a vulgar person." 大切な言葉ですね。

（一口アドバイス）56　Thank you for being my friend.

225

refugee

[rèfjudʒíː]

Noun　　Academic

Def : a person who leaves his or her country to flee from danger and find safety in another country

日 : 難民

Syn : exile, displaced person, evacuee

e. g. : The UN is an agency responsible for helping **refugees**. (国連は難民を助ける責任ある機関である)

Notes : 国際情勢を知るのに重要な単語です。その他、refugee camps（難民キャンプ）は日本語でもよく知られています。

226

grasp

[grǽsp]

Verb　　Conversation

Def : take hold of something firmly with your hand; comprehend

日 : しっかりとつかむ、理解する

Syn : understand

e. g. : His story was very difficult to **grasp**. (彼の話は分かりづらかった)

Notes : I grasped the opportunity.（機会をつかんだ）のようにも使います。またこの語は have や understand などと同じで、進行形では使いません。注意しましょう。

227

allure

[əlúər]

Noun　　Basic

Def : an attractive quality

日 : 魅了

Syn : charm, enchantment

e. g. : He gave himself up to the queen's **allure**. (女王の魅力に彼は心を奪われた)

Notes : 次の説明のように動詞としても使うことができます。A fancy word used to mean attractive, such as "alluring." It is a very chic（上品で）and sophisticated word to use.

228

persevere

[pɜ̀ːrsəvíər]

Verb　　Basic

Def : continue to do something, even if it is difficult

日 : 根気よくやり通す

Syn : keep trying, persist

e. g. : You have to **persevere**, if you want to succeed. (成功しようと思えば頑張らなくてはいけないよ)

Notes : 頑張る is a very important word for Japanese people and an important concept too. Persevere has the same meaning although we don't use it as much as Japanese people use 頑張る. We do not shout "Persevere!" However, it is the perfect word for longer sentences talking about effort.「頑張る」を英語に翻訳する際に使ってみましょう。

（一口アドバイス）57　Be lowly wise. (John Milton)

229 mundane

[mʌndéɪn]

Adjective　Basic

Def : ordinary and uninteresting, dull

日 : 日常の

Syn : common, everyday

e. g. : Making photocopies is one of the most **mundane** tasks in the office. （コピー取りは一番ありふれた事務作業だ）

Notes : mundane の語源は「世界」「世間」「世俗」を意味するラテン語の "mundus" から来ています。英語の語源を知ることでその意味がつかみやすくなります。語源を自分で調べてみましょう。

---

230 double

[dʌ́b(ə)l]

Adjective　Culture

Def : being binational and/or bicultural

日 : 日本語で「ハーフ」という表現に代わって使われるようになっている

Syn : biracial, bicultural

e. g. : Children who are "**double**" have the wonderful advantages of knowing two different cultures, and in some cases, two different languages. （「ダブル」の子供には2つの文化、時に2つの言語を知っているという強みがある）

Notes : In other parts of the world bicultural people use the term "double," as it does not include negative connotations of being just "half" of one culture and one half of another, but rather being composed of two whole cultures with a double advantage. 「ハーフ」ではなくて「ダブル」を使いましょう。

---

231 attribute (to)

[ətríbjuːt]

Verb　Communication

Def : believe that one thing caused another

日 : 〜のせいにする

Syn : ascribe, impute

e. g. : I **attribute** Mary's bad temper to all the problems she's been having lately. （メアリーの不機嫌は最近彼女がかかえている問題のせいだと思う）

Notes : In communication theory and in psychology, we sometimes talk about Attribution Theory, which has to do with how we explain our own behavior and the behavior of others. 行動の原因を何に求めるかについての理論を「帰属理論」といいます。

---

232 counterpart

[káuntərpàːrt]

Noun　Basic

Def : someone with the same job or who is in the same situation, as someone in a different place

日 : よく似た人（もの）、〜に当たる人

Syn : fellow, equivalent

e. g. : Our prime minister is the **counterpart** of your president. （我々の首相はあなた方の大統領に当たる）

Notes : counterpart がないケースも多いですね。服などの色が渋いと言っても、「渋い」にぴったりの英語は思い当たりません。英語の facade なども適当な訳がなく、最近では、そのような単語をカタカナ表記で訳すことが多いです。

（一ロアドバイス）58　偶儻不羈（てきとうふき）なる書生（新島襄）

233

"Please do as you see fit."

[plíːz dúː / əz_ju síː fít]

Other　　Conversation

Def : as you like

日 : 適当にしてください

Syn : as you think best

e.g. : If there is no particular way to do something, just do **as you see fit**. (特別なやり方がないのなら、適当にやってください)

Notes : 適当に is one of those really useful Japanese expressions. This is one good way, I think, to say it in English. 便利ですね。

234

furious

[fjúəriəs]

Adjective　　Conversation

Def : extremely angry

日 : ひどく怒った、激怒した

Syn : very angry, raging

e.g. : My father was **furious** with me for being late. (父は私が時間に遅れたことに激怒した)

Notes : All students know the word "angry," but we use "furious" a lot too. Notice that you say "angry/furious WITH someone." with をお忘れなく。/f/ の音にメラメラと炎のように見えるほどの怒りが表れているように思えます。

235

"I mean it."

[aɪ míːn_ɪt]

Verb　　Conversation

Def : be not joking

日 : 本気である

Syn : be serious

e.g. : "You have to give a presentation in English." "Are you joking?" "No, **I mean it**." (「英語でプレゼンテーションをしてください」「からかっているのですか」「いいえ、本気ですよ」)

Notes : 会話でよく使われる表現です。主語を I 以外にすることもできます。"She means it." (彼女は本気です)、また「信じてよ」と訳すこともできます。

236

connotation

[kὰːnətéɪʃən]

Noun　　Literature

Def : an idea suggested by a word in addition to its basic meaning

日 : 含意（表に出ていない隠された意味）

Syn : implication, hidden meaning

e.g. : To understand this poem, you must grasp the **connotation** of the word "eagle." (この詩を理解するためには、「鷹」という語の含意を読み取る必要がある)

Notes : 文学表現は言葉の表面上の意味だけではなく、その向こう側にある深層が見えないと十分に楽しめないことがあります。一つ一つの言葉の "connotation" を考えてみましょう。ちなみに表面上の意味は "denotation" です。

（一口アドバイス）59　If you don't believe in yourself, no one will.

237

socialize

[sóuʃəlàɪz]

Verb　Communication

Def :	to spend a pleasurable time with other people
日 :	付き合う
Syn :	get together, hang out, hang around with

e. g. : I enjoyed **socializing** with my colleagues.（同僚との交流を楽しんだ）

Notes : It is important for college students to learn, but college is also an opportunity to make new friends and spend time with them. 大学でも同僚や友人と一緒に時間を過ごすことは重要です。かつてボーリングを通してそのような交流が図られました。今はカラオケ？

238

lead role

[líːd róul]

Noun　Literature

Def :	the main character in a movie or play
日 :	主人公
Syn :	main part, the lead

e. g. : I hope to get the **lead role** in the Shakespeare drama performance this year.（今年のシェイクスピア劇では主役をやりたいな）

Notes : Necessary to talk about theater. 演劇関係では必要な用語ですね。主役も大事ですが、脇役（supporting role）や大道具係（flyman）、照明係（lighting technician）などの裏方（background role）の仕事も重要です。

239

eliminate

[ɪlímənèɪt]

Verb　Current

Def :	remove someone or something not wanted or needed
日 :	排除する
Syn :	get rid of, rule out

e. g. : You should **eliminate** negative ways of thinking.（ネガティブな考え方は排除すべきだ）

Notes : 排除する対象は、不安から差別、ドラッグまで多様なものをあてはめることができます（eliminate anxiety, discrimination, drugs）。

240

vomit

[vάːmət]

Verb　Basic

Def :	the act of the contents of the stomach leaving your body through your mouth
日 :	吐く
Syn :	throw up

e. g. : Some people **vomited** as the result of drinking too much alcohol at the party.（コンパでお酒を飲み過ぎて、何人かは戻してしまった）

Notes : 例文のような場合以外にも、外国で子供を病院に連れて行った際には、Did he vomit?（嘔吐しましたか）などの質問をされることがあります。

（一口アドバイス）60　You've got to accentuate the positive, eliminate the negative. (Johnny Mercer)

241 considerate

[kənsídərət]

Adjective   Conversation

Def : kind, helpful
日 : 思いやりのある
Syn : thoughtful

e.g. : The nurses were very **considerate** and thoughtful. (看護師はとても思いやりがあり思慮深かった)

Notes : A useful word to use when receiving a gift: "How considerate! Thank you so much!" お礼を言う際に使いましょう。

---

242 vulgar

[vΛlgər]

Adjective   Current

Def : in bad taste
日 : 品が無い、下品
Syn : coarse, crude, low-class

e.g. : I can't stand him. He's so **vulgar**. (もう彼には堪えられない。品がなさ過ぎる)

Notes : Useful for talking about art and people. The opposite of "sophisticated" or "refined." 人の描写にも使えますね。

---

243 desert

[dɪzə́ːrt]

Verb   Basic

Def : cruelly or irresponsibly leave someone
日 : 見捨てる
Syn : abandon, leave

e.g. : Do not **desert** me, Gabriel! (ゲイブリエル、私を見捨てないでちょうだい！) (Hardy, 1874)

Notes : desert「見捨てる」という単語、どんなときに使うのだろうと思っていましたが、このような時に使えるのですね。名詞で使うと「砂漠」で強勢は前に、食後のデザートは dessert で s が 2 つあり、強勢も後ろの音節につきます。

---

244 verbatim

[vərbéɪtəm]

Adverb   Academic

Def : in exactly the same words
日 : 逐語的に，言葉どおりに
Syn : literally

e.g. : I repeated what he said **verbatim**. (彼の発言を言葉どおりに繰り返した)

Notes : 発音に注意しましょう。後半の a に強勢がつき、しかも /ei/ と読みます。

(一口アドバイス) 61   I have a dream today. (Martin Luther King Jr.)

245 gorgeous

[gɔ́ːrdʒəs]

Adjective　Conversation

Def: extremely nice, beautiful or pleasant

日: 素晴らしい、見事な

Syn: attractive

e.g.: What **gorgeous** weather we have today!（今日はなんて素晴らしい天気なんでしょう！）

Notes: 梅雨前の、新緑の輝く5月の天気を表現するのに最適です。もちろん、She is gorgeous.（彼女は華麗だ）のように使うこともお忘れなく。

---

246 illegal

[ɪlíːg(ə)l]

Adjective　Basic

Def: not allowed by law

日: 不法な

Syn: unlawful, criminal

e.g.: There are many **illegal** workers in that town.（その街には不法就労者が多くいる）

Notes: 反意語は legal ですが、legal wife（正妻）のようにも使われます。

---

247 figurehead

[fíɡjərhèd]

Noun　Conversation

Def: a visible leader of an organization, who actually has no real power

日: （名目上の）リーダー

Syn: symbolic leader

e.g.: Masaaki has such a strong personality that he doesn't want to be a mere **figurehead**.（正章は非常に強い個性をもっているので、単なる名目上のリーダーにはなりたくない）

Notes: "figurehead" とは、もともと「船首像」（船の舳先につけた大きなお守り）のことです。最前に立つ飾りなので「名目上のリーダー」を表すようになったのでしょう。

---

248 corpus

[kɔ́ːrpəs]

Noun　Linguistics

Def: a database of words in electronic form

日: 単語を集めたデータベース、体（からだ）

Syn: collection

e.g.: This dictionary has been based on a 100-word **corpus** of British English.（この辞書はイギリス英語で最もよく使われる100語をもとにしています）

Notes: Corpus linguistics is the study of large amounts of language examples and can help us understand how a language actually works. コーパス言語学によって実際の言葉の使い方がわかります。

（一口アドバイス）62　日本語力を高めると外国語も上達する。

249 dictator

[díkteıtər]

Noun　Basic

Def : a leader who has total power
日 : 独裁者
Syn : tyrant

e.g. : The **dictator** commanded his men to invade neighboring countries. (その独裁者は、近隣諸国を侵略せよと部下に命じた)

Notes : 「独裁国家」は "dictatorship" です。チャップリンの The Great Dictator (『独裁者』、1940 年制作) は必見の映画です。特に最後の演説は英語を勉強していてよかったと思える部分です。まだ見ていない人は是非見てみましょう。

---

250 definition

[dèfəníʃən]

Noun　Academic

Def : an explanation of the meaning of a word or phrase
日 : 定義
Syn : explanation, description

e.g. : In your graduation thesis, you need to first show the **definitions** of the important terms. (卒論では最初に重要な用語の定義を提示する必要がある)

Notes : 定義と聞くと堅苦しく感じるかもしれませんが、実際に卒論を書く際には重要な用語について学問的に説明する必要があります。英英辞典をみると用語の定義がわかりやすく書いてあるので参考になります。ちなみに、難しいのは目に見えないものの定義。love (愛), motivation (学習動機), intelligence (知能) などはどのように定義できるでしょうか。

---

251 exhausted

[ıgzɔ́:stıd]

Adjective　Basic

Def : extremely tired
日 : 疲れ果てた
Syn : worn out

e.g. : After the marathon, I was completely **exhausted**. (マラソンの後、すっかり疲れ果ててしまった)

Notes : All my students know the word "tired," but I never hear them say "exhausted," although native English speakers use this word a lot. 「疲れた」という時に使ってみましょう。

---

252 ingredient

[ıngrí:dıənt]

Noun　Basic

Def : something that is used to make a food, product, etc.
日 : 材料、要素、成分
Syn : element

e.g. : Clothes seemed at this early time of his love a necessary **ingredient** of the sweet mixture called Bathsheba Everdene. (恋心の初期の段階では、彼にとっては、洋服はバスシバ・エヴァディーンという甘い混合物を愛しく思うための必要な成分であるようだ) (Hardy, 1874)

Notes : この単語は料理のレシピ、例えば、日本料理の食材 (ingredients in Japanese cuisine) でよく使う単語ですが、こういう比喩的な表現でも使うのですね。

(一口アドバイス) 63　If you don't make mistakes, you won't make anything!

253

learner autonomy

[lɔ́ːrnər ɔːtɑ́ːnəmi]

Noun   Academic

Def : being responsible for one's own learning

日 : 学習者の自立性

Syn : autonomous learning

e. g. : Learner autonomy is something important for people to understand not only as language learners but throughout their entire lives.（自立的に学ぶことは言語学習だけでなく生涯に渉って重要だ）

Notes : To be autonomous in language learning means being responsible by knowing what one is learning and why, and how one will use that information in the future. 自立的に学ぶことの重要性を再認識したいですね。

254

adjacent

[ədʒéɪs(ə)nt]

Adjective   Academic

Def : next to

日 : 近隣の、隣接した

Syn : neighboring

e. g. : There is a parking lot **adjacent** to the building.（その建物に隣接して駐車場がある）

Notes : This vocabulary item is also used academically in math and science. 数学や理科でも使われるのですね。また宝くじの前後賞の前後という場合にも adjacent numbers のように使われます。

255

synthesize

[sínθəsàɪz]

Verb   Academic

Def : put separate facts, ideas or pieces of information together to form something new

日 : 総合する

Syn : incorporate, integrate

e. g. : The student used two different pieces of evidence and **synthesized** them to create a strong argument.（学生は２つの根拠をあわせて説得力のある主張を作り上げた）

Notes : Synthesis of ideas shows advanced critical thinking skills. It shows that the writer has completely understood a concept and can integrate the idea into her existing knowledge. よくわかっていないとどの概念と結びつけるかわかりません。深い理解を！

256

communicative competence

[kəmjúːnɪkətɪv kɑ́ːmpət(ə)ns]

Noun   Communication

Def : the ability and skills to communicate

日 : コミュニケーション能力

Syn : communicative proficiency

e. g. : To have **communicative competence** takes more than just knowing grammar; you have to know what you can say in a particular circumstance.（コミュニケーション能力を身につけるには文法を知っているだけでなく、ある状況で何を言うことができるか知っておく必要もある）

Notes : As students of language, we must develop communicative competence rather than just learn grammar and vocabulary. 語彙、文法も重要なのですが、コミュニケーションの中で使えないといけませんね。

（一口アドバイス）64　内省のない人に向上はない。

257

theme
[θíːm]

Noun　Conversation

Def : the main topic of discussion or writing

日 : テーマ

Syn : subject, main idea, topic

e. g. : There's an exhibition on the **theme** of flowers. (花がテーマの展覧会が開かれている)

Notes : 日本語では「テーマ」と呼んでいます。「テーマパーク」や「テーマソング」としても日常的に使っています。発音に気をつけましょう。

258

coming out
[kʌ́mɪŋ_áut]

Other　Current

Def : publicly announcing one's sexual identity to the public

日 : 同性愛者であることを公表すること

Syn : confessing or announcing your homosexuality

e. g. : For some LGBTQ youth, **coming out** of the closet is very difficult because they fear what their family and friends will think about them. (性的少数者グループの若者にとってその公表は家族や友人がどう思うか心配なだけになかなかできない)

Notes : The LGBTQ community is not something new, but we are seeing more awareness and acceptance of this minority group in society. 日本語の「カミングアウト」はいろいろな状況で使われますが、英語では同性愛についてのみ使われることに気をつけましょう。詳細は LGBTQ（No. 47）を参照して下さい。

259

kinesics
[kɪníːsɪks]

Noun　Communication

Def : communication using body movement, including gestures

日 : 動作学

Syn : NA

e. g. : **Kinesics** is different in different cultures. （文化によって動作は異なる）

Notes : It is important for language learners to learn about nonverbal communication, including gestures and body movements. ジェスチャーや体の動きがどのようなメッセージを伝えるかを学ぶのが動作学です。

260

allocate
[ǽləkèɪt]

Verb　Academic

Def : give a share of something (e.g. food, money) for a particular purpose

日 : 分配する

Syn : assign, distribute

e. g. : I think schools should **allocate** more lesson time to moral education. （学校は道徳の授業を増やした方がいいと思う）

Notes : 大学のシラバスには評価規準が記載してありますが、その記述には、A weight of 50% will be allocated to the final test.（最終テストのウエートは50%です）のように allocate を使った記載がしてあります。

（一口アドバイス）65　Rejoice always, pray continually, give thanks in all circumstances（聖書：テサロニケ人への手紙）.

261

permit

[pɔ́ːmɪt]

Noun   TOEIC

Def : an official certificate that allows you to do something

日 : 許可証

Syn : license (US), licence (UK)

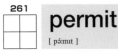

e.g. : I noticed that the **permit** had expired. (許可証の期限が切れていることに気付いた)

Notes : 「運転免許証」が "driving license" なのに対して、「国際運転免許証」は "International Driving Permit (IDP)" といいます。これは、それ自体で運転免許証とはならず、あくまでも本来の運転免許証に付随する「許可証」という意味合いだからです。

262

liability

[làɪəbíləti]

Noun   TOEIC

Def : the duty of a person, business, or organization to pay for something

日 : 法的責任

Syn : debt

e.g. : The company has **liability** for the damage. (会社には損害に対する責任がある)

Notes : "be liable to～" は「～しがちである」「～する傾向にある」という意味です。"be likely to～" が良いことにも悪いことにも用いられるのに対して、"be liable to～" はネガティブな意味合いで用いられるので気をつけましょう。

263

cozy

[kóuzi]

Adjective   Basic

Def : comfortable and warm

日 : 居心地の良い

Syn : comfortable

e.g. : The old couple lived in a **cozy** little house. (その老夫婦はこじんまりした居心地の良い家に住んでいた)

Notes : "cozy" はただ居心地が良いだけではなく、こじんまりとして暖かい雰囲気を表します。また、なれ合い (cozy relationship) のようにも使われます。

264

amiable

[éɪmɪəb(ə)l]

Adjective   Basic

Def : pleasant, open and friendly

日 : 優しい、愛想の良い、友好的な、気立ての良い

Syn : friendly, affable, genial

e.g. : The classroom atmosphere was relaxed and **amiable**. (そのクラスは打ち解けて友好的な雰囲気だった)

Notes : A good alternative for describing a friendly or nice person. "friendly" 以外の「友好的な、気さくな」を意味する単語を次の例文のように覚えましょう。She is so amiable! How can you dislike her? 発音にも気をつけましょう。

（一口アドバイス）66　Do, or do not. There is no try. (Yoda, *Star Wars*)

265

vulnerable

[vʌ́lnərəb(ə)l]

Adjective　TOEIC

Def : easily hurt, influenced, or attacked

日 : 脆弱な

Syn : unsafe, helpless

e.g. : Do you know how **vulnerable** you are here? (ここでは君の立場がいかに脆弱なものかわかっていますか)

Notes : その他、ビジネスで vulnerable to a take-over (会社の乗っ取りに弱い) などとも使われます。名詞形は vulnerability (脆弱性) です。

266

revenue

[révən(j)ùː]

Noun　TOEIC

Def : income that a business or government receives regularly

日 : 歳入、収益

Syn : received payment

e.g. : This graph shows the amount of tourism **revenue**. (このグラフは観光収入の額を示しています)

Notes : A word used when talking about govern-ment taxes. 政府の収入の合計を表すほか、企業の収益、例えば advertising revenue (広告収入) のようにも使われます。

267

donate

[dóuneɪt]

Verb　Basic

Def : give goods or money to a needy person or organi-zation

日 : 寄付する

Syn : contribute, give

e.g. : Every Christmas, Professor Morita **donates** money to a local chari-ty. (毎年クリスマスに、森田教授は地元の慈善団体に寄付をする)

Notes : 血液や臓器の提供者を donor といいますね。名詞は donation (寄付、寄贈) です。

268

plagiarism

[pléɪdʒərìzm]

Noun　Academic

Def : using someone else's ideas without acknowledging the source

日 : 剽窃

Syn : stealing

e.g. : The student was ashamed when her **plagiarism** was discovered. (その学生は、剽窃が見つかりはずかしい思いをした)

Notes : Plagiarism can be easily avoided by in-cluding references to every idea that you use in your work. When you write a paper, you can use other people's ideas, but you need to express them in your own words. If you use someone else's words as your own, you are guilty of plagia-rism. 自分で書いたものと人が書いたものを区別しましょう。

(一口アドバイス) 67　Where's the editorial responsibility in not publishing them? (Mike, *Spotlight*)

269 stereotype

[stériətàɪp]

Noun　Basic

Def : a common fixed idea or assumption about someone or something

日 : 固定観念

Syn : fixed idea

e.g. : Today, most people don't support the **stereotype** of women as weak. (今日では「女性は弱い」という固定観念を支持しない人がほとんどだ)

Notes : 世の中には多種多様な固定観念がありますが、それに惑わされない、広い視野をもちたいものです。

---

270 adorable

[ədɔ́:rəb(ə)l]

Adjective　Basic

Def : extremely cute

日 : 可愛い

Syn : sweet, lovely, cute

e.g. : My sister's baby is **adorable**. (姉の赤ちゃんはとってもかわいい)

Notes : 「かわいい」は最近英語でそのままつかわれますが、cute 以外の言い方として adorable も覚えておきましょう。A good alternative to "cute," which sounds a little childish. Adorable is a much better word. 例えば、"Look at that puppy! How adorable!" のように。

---

271 conspiracy

[kənspírəsi]

Noun　TOEIC

Def : a secret plan made by a group of people to do something illegal

日 : 陰謀

Syn : plot, scheme

e.g. : In the play, the hero becomes involved in a **conspiracy**. (劇中で主人公は陰謀に巻き込まれる)

Notes : シェイクスピア劇には「陰謀」をたくらむ人物がたくさん登場します。

---

272 have butterflies in one's stomach

[hæv bʌ́tərflaɪz / ɪn wʌnz stʌ́mək]

Idiom　Basic

Def : be anxious about a performance

日 : 緊張して落ち着かない

Syn : be nervous

e.g. : Even veteran actors often **have butterflies in their stomach** before going on stage. (ベテランの俳優でさえ、舞台に出る前にとても緊張する)

Notes : 日本人としてこの言葉が表す状況に置かれることが多いですね。いつも使う nervous (I am nervous about the presentation tomorrow.) ばかりではなく、この言葉を代わりに使ってみましょう。one's のところに人称代名詞の所有格をいれます。

（一口アドバイス）68　この一球は絶対無二の一球なり、されば身心をあげて一打すべし。（福田雅之助）

273

inaugurate

[ɪnɔ́:gjərèɪt]

Verb　TOEIC

Def : put someone into a new position (e.g. president) with a ceremony

日 : (人)を就任させる

Syn : install

e.g. : John F. Kennedy was **inaugurated** as the 35th President of the United States. （ジョン・F・ケネディは第35代アメリカ合衆国大統領に就任した）

Notes : inaugurate はラテン語の "inaugurare"（「占う」）から来ています。誰が次期アメリカ大統領になるかは世界的な関心事ですね。JFK (John F. Kennedy) については暗殺の真相について未だに議論がつきません（映画『JFK』 オリヴァー・ストーン監督、1991年公開などを参照）。

274

persuasion

[pərswéɪʒən]

Noun　Basic

Def : the act of changing someone's opinion or getting someone to do something

日 : 説得

Syn : conviction

e.g. : He did not change his mind in spite of all kinds of **persuasion** from his family. （彼は家族がどれほど説得しても考えを変えなかった）

Notes : Jane Austen の小説 Persuasion（邦題は『説得』、『説きふせられて』）は、周りに説得されて婚約を解消した恋人たちが再びよりを戻す物語。まだ読んでいない人は是非ご一読を。

275

moody

[mu:di]

Adjective　Conversation

Def : being unhappy, angry or irritated, seemingly without valid reason

日 : 不機嫌な、きまぐれな

Syn : cross, sulky

e.g. : She was extremely **moody** when I called her. （電話した時、彼女はとても不機嫌だった）

Notes : テレビなどでタレントなどが安易に口にする「ムーディー」。これをそのまま英語として使うと、とんでもないことになるので気をつけましょう。「ムードのある」という意味ではないので注意が必要です。

276

feminism

[fémənìzm]

Noun　Basic

Def : the belief that men and women should have equal rights and opportunities

日 : フェミニズム

Syn : advocacy of women's rights

e.g. : **Feminism** has become a worldwide movement. （フェミニズムは世界中で活発になっている）

Notes : Japanese students may associate the word "feminism" just with female followers of this movement, when in reality, many men also share feminist beliefs. フェミニズムは男性の問題でもあります。

（一口アドバイス）69　Rome was not built in a day.

277 gist

[dʒíst]

Noun　Current

Def : overall meaning or idea

日 : 要点、要旨

Syn : essence

e.g. : I didn't get every word, but I understood the **gist** of it.（全部は聞き取れなかったが、要点はつかんだ）

Notes : Notice that the "g" is pronounced like "j." 発音に気をつけましょう。

278 "How bothersome!"

[hâu bɑ́:ðərsəm]

Other　Conversation

Def : An expression for when something is troublesome, time-consuming or difficult.

日 : 面倒な

Syn : How troublesome! What a hassle!

e.g. : "I have to take off my shoes again?! Really? **How bothersome!**"（また靴を脱ぐの？何て面倒な！）

Notes : In Britain, we use the expression "What a hassle!" a lot. But "bothersome" or "troublesome" are used everywhere. 面倒、ということは多いですね。会話で使ってみましょう。

279 tangible

[tǽndʒəb(ə)l]

Adjective　Basic

Def : real and not imaginary; able to be seen or touched

日 : 触ることのできる、理解できる

Syn : touchable

e.g. : There has been a **tangible** decline in the grammatical knowledge of recent English Department students.（近年英語英文学科学生の文法能力に明らかな低下がみられる）

Notes : tangible は使い道の多い単語で、例えば tangible cultural properties（有形文化財）や tangible results（目に見える結果）のように使うことができます。

280 geek

[ɡíːk]

Noun　Current

Def : someone who likes a particular subject a lot（and is not usually fashionable）

日 : おたく、マニア

Syn : super-fan

e.g. : As for American comics, I admit I'm a sort of **geek**. Ask me anything about Superman, or Green Lantern, if you like.（アメコミに関しちゃ、俺、ちょっとしたオタクだから。スーパーマンでも、何ならグリーン・ランタンでもいいよ、なんでも訊いてみて）

Notes : 日本でも「オタク」という言葉からネガティブな印象がなくなってきましたが、アメリカでの "geek" も同様。今では皆と一緒より、むしろ何かについて "geek" なほうがクールといった雰囲気です。"geek out"（オタク話で盛り上がる）といった風に動詞で使うことも。

（一口アドバイス）70　ノンネイティブのゴールは 8000 語。

281

recruit

[rɪkrúːt]

Verb　TOEIC

Def : find new members for an organization

日 : （仕事に人を）募集する

Syn : hire

e.g. : In spring, most Japanese companies start to **recruit** recent college graduates. (春になるとほとんどの日本の企業は新卒大学生の採用をはじめる)

Notes : リクルートというカタカナでお馴染みの言葉ですが、名詞で使うと、新入社員（recruit）という意味になります。

282

conflict

[kάːnflɪkt]

Noun　Basic

Def : disagreement, argument, or fight

日 : 葛藤、確執、対立

Syn : dispute, disagreement, fighting

e.g. : She feels **conflict** between her work and her family obligations. (彼女は仕事と家庭の義務との間に葛藤を抱えている)

Notes : 文学では、主人公が「心の葛藤」を抱く場面がよく描かれます。

283

drawback

[drɔ́ːbæk]

Noun　Communication

Def : a problem, disadvantage, or negative effect

日 : 欠点

Syn : weakness, downside

e.g. : The plan has a **drawback** we need to overcome. (その計画に欠点があり、それをなんとかしないといけません)

Notes : 欠点というと bad point や demerit を使いがちですが、drawback も同じ意味です。「後ろへ下がる、手を引く」から「欠点」になるとは面白いですね。一長一短（drawback and advantage）。

284

superficial

[sùːpərfíʃəl]

Adjective　Basic

Def : of minor importance; not true, genuine or real

日 : 表面的な

Syn : shallow

e.g. : He smiles and seems friendly, but it is just **superficial**. (彼はにこやかで好意的に映るがそれは見せかけだけだ)

Notes : Useful to talk about people's characters and about knowledge too. The opposite of "deep" or "genuine." 人の描写はエッセイや英語日記に必要ですね。

（一口アドバイス）71　Tell me your story. I'll tell you mine.

285

bully

[búli]

Verb　Basic

Def : frighten someone who is smaller or weaker

日 : いじめる

Syn : harass, intimidate

e.g. : She was **bullied** by some older girls. (上級生によって彼女はいじめられていた)

Notes : The act of bullying can occur not only in school but also in the workplace. いじめは学校だけでなく職場でも起こり得ることです。この単語は動詞でも名詞でも使われます。その場合にはいじめっこ（school bully、学校でのいじめっこ）という意味になります。いじめ自体は bullying とします。

286

compromise

[kάːmprəmàɪz]

Noun　Basic

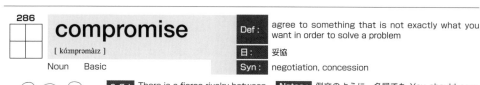

✕ about meat

Def : agree to something that is not exactly what you want in order to solve a problem

日 : 妥協

Syn : negotiation, concession

e.g. : There is a fierce rivalry between Tom and Tadashi. A **compromise** would be impossible. (トムと正はものすごく張り合っている。妥協は無理だろう)

Notes : 例文のように、名詞でも You should compromise. (妥協すべきだ) のように動詞でも使うことができます。

287

segment

[ségmənt]

Verb　Academic

Def : divide into parts

日 : 分割する

Syn : divide

e.g. : The Applied Linguistics course is **segmented** into three parts. (この応用言語学のコースは３つの部分に分かれています)

Notes : divide でいいのですが、大学などのシラバスなどではこのような正式な表現が使われることが多いです。私が最初に見たのは 2000 年のトロント大学の Cumming 教授の評価法のシラバス。この言葉を使うと簡潔に表現される印象になりますね。名詞としても使うことができます。

288

fringe

[fríndʒ]

Noun　Conversation

Def : outer edge; radical, not mainstream; front

日 : へり

Syn : outskirts

e.g. : Homeless people feel they are on the **fringes** of society. (ホームレスの人達は社会の片隅に追いやられていると感じている)

Notes : Often used in the plural. fringe benefits というと給料以外に従業員に支払われる諸手当を指します。

（一口アドバイス）72　自分がつまらなく思えたときは、非常に進歩したときだ。

289 enhance

[ɪnhǽns]

Verb　Basic

Def : improve something that's already good

日 : 高める

Syn : improve, enrich

e. g. : Vending machines don't **enhance** the landscape. (自動販売機は街の景観をよくするものではない)

Notes : This is a lovely word you can use in talking about everything from cooking (herbs enhance flavor) to studying (reading enhances vocabulary) to job-hunting (how to enhance your chance of success). 使い道が広そうですね。

---

290 good and evil

[gúd_ən_íːvəl]

Noun　Literature

Def : right and wrong

日 : 善悪

Syn : right and wrong

e. g. : The battle between **good and evil** is one of the main themes of fantasy literature. (善悪の戦いは、ファンタジー文学の主要テーマのひとつだ)

Notes : 聖書の創世記 (Genesis) でアダムとイヴが神のタブーを破って食すのは、リンゴではなく、「善悪を知る知識の木」(the tree of knowledge of good and evil) の果実です (Cf. 第2章9節)。

---

291 simile

[símɪli]

Noun　Linguistics

Def : an expression that compares two things, using "like" or "as"

日 : 直喩

Syn : NA

e. g. : "The surface of the lake was like a mirror" is a **simile**. (湖の表面はまるで鏡のようだった、というのは直喩です)

Notes : Using similes can make your writing more vivid. エッセイを書く際には是非使ってみましょう。

---

292 "What a shame!"

[(h)wʌ̃t_ə ʃéɪm]

Other　Conversation

Def : How disappointing!

日 : 残念ですね。

Syn : What a pity! That's a shame. Oh, shame!

e. g. : "You can't come to the party? Oh, **what a shame!**" (パーティーに来れない？それは残念だ)

Notes : Students tend to know only one meaning of the word, "shame": 恥ずかしさ. Indeed we can use that word in expressions like "Shame on you!" (恥を知れ！) or "Have you no shame?" (恥ないのか！) However, more commonly we use the word in expressions of regret. "What a shame!" or even just "Shame!" means「残念！」使ってみましょう。

(一口アドバイス) 73　We can feed this mind of ours in a wise passiveness. (William Wordsworth)

the pros and cons

[ðə próuz_ən_kɔ́nz]

Noun　Academic

Def : the advantages and disadvantages

日 : 長所と短所、功罪

Syn : merits and demerits

e. g. : "Okay, let's discuss **the pros and cons** of their new suggestion." (じゃあ、彼らの新しい提案のいい点と悪い点について話し合いましょう)

Notes : 英語コミュニケーションでは論理性に支えられた説得力が重視されます。どんな事柄でも、正負両面から検討する、そういった場面で登場するのがこのフレーズ。議論の始めにこの言葉を口にすると、「場を仕切っている」感を味わえます。

---

intrinsic

[ɪntrínsɪk]

Adjective　TOEIC

Def : related to the core nature of a thing; built-in

日 : 本来の、内在する

Syn : inherent

e. g. : Professor Fukumoto told us that war is not **intrinsic** to human nature. (福本教授は、人は本来、戦争をするようには生まれついていないと言った)

Notes : intrinsic の同意語には、同じく "in-" で始まる "inborn"、"innate" などがあります。また英語が好きだから英語を学ぶという動機づけの種類を内発的動機づけ (intrinsic motivation) といいます。

---

endorse

[ɪndɔ́ːrs]

Verb　Academic

Def : sign (a check) on the back

日 : 小切手に裏書きする、支持する

Syn : sign

e. g. : "**Endorse** here" means you are required to sign. (「ここに裏書きしてください」とあれば、署名が求められています)

Notes : 留学中に checkbook (小切手帳) を持ち、そこで覚えた単語です。小切手をもらった人は銀行に持って行って、裏に自分の名前をサインをして自分が受け取ったことを証明します。

---

may as well

[mèɪ əz wél]

Other　Literature

Def : used to suggest doing something, without much enthusiasm

日 : 〜しても当然、〜したほうがよい

Syn : might as well, should

e. g. : The poor woman's dead, and you can't bring her to life, and you **may as well** sit down comfortable, and finish another with us. (あの女は死んでしまったし、もう生きるかえりゃしない。だから、座ってもう一杯飲んだらええ) (Hardy, 1874)

Notes : 例えば、Because the professor extended the deadline for the final report, we may as well (should) start working on it now. (先生がレポートの締めきりを延ばしてくれたのだから、すぐに取りかかる方がよい) のように使うことができます。この場合、may as well の代わりに should を使ったり、... it would be a good idea for us to start working on it now. のように書き換えることも可能です。日記やエッセイで利用しましょう。

---

297 expository

[ɪkspɑ́ːzətɔ̀ːri]

Adjective Academic

Def : explaining or describing something

日 : 説明文の

Syn : explanatory

e. g. : When you read an **expository** text, pay attention to the topic sentence of each paragraph. (説明文を読む時はトピックセンテンスに注意して読みなさい)

Notes : 論説文の場合にはスキミング（ざっと読む）とスキャニング（特定の情報を探しながら読む）、この2つのストラテジーが有効です。物語文の場合には飛ばし読みをせず情景を思い浮かべながらじっくりと読むことが大切です。ジャンルによって使うストラテジーを変えることが重要です。

---

298 gadget

[gǽdʒɪt]

Noun Communication

Def : a small device that does a particular job, e.g. a remote control

日 : 便利なおしゃれツール

Syn : tool, device

e. g. : Nick's hobby is collecting stylish kitchen **gadgets**. (ニックの趣味はおしゃれなキッチン用品を集めることだ)

Notes : あるリスニングのテキストの中に "gadget sound" というユニットがあり、音を聞き、それが何の道具の音かを答える問題がありました。変なユニットだなと思っていたら、改訂版ではそのユニットは消えていました。

---

299 abstract

[æbstrǽkt]

Adjective Academic

Def : relating to ideas and not real or concrete things

日 : 抽象的

Syn : notional, conceptual

e. g. : That explanation is a bit too **abstract** for me. (その説明は少し抽象的すぎた)

Notes : Useful for describing ideas. 名詞で使われると論文などの「要約」という意味になります。その場合、強勢が前の音節におかれるので気をつけましょう。

---

300 invaluable

[ɪnvǽljuəb(ə)l]

Adjective Basic

Def : priceless or of great worth

日 : 貴重な

Syn : vital, helpful

e. g. : The letter is **invaluable** as a historical document. (その手紙は歴史資料として大変貴重なものだ)

Notes : in がつくと反対の意味になりそうですが、そうならない単語があるので注意しましょう。例えば、different（違う）と indifferent（無関心の）など。

（一口アドバイス）75 Be prepared. Luck is truly where preparation meets opportunity. (Randy Pausch)

Part 4

Accomplishment

The greatest accomplishment is not in never falling.

but in rising again after you fall.

(Vince Lombardi, football coach, from Myers & Burnett, 1971)

A great accomplishment shouldn't be the end of the road, just the starting point

for the next leap forward.

(Harvey Mackay, 1999, businessman and author)

Myers, H., Burnett, R. (1971). *Vincent Lombardi: Young football coach*. Bobbs-Merrill Company.

Mackay, H. (1999). *Dig your well before you're thirsty: The only networking book you'll ever need*. Crown.

301

banality of evil

[bənǽləti əv_íːv(ə)l]

Phrase   Communication

Def : the idea that evil things could be done by average people

日 : 悪の凡庸さ（陳腐さ）

Syn : NA

e. g. : Hannah Arendt proposed the idea of "**banality of evil**" in relation to the crimes of the Nazis.（ハンナ・アーレントはナチスの犯罪に関して、「悪の陳腐さ」という概念を提唱した）

Notes : とても難しい単語ですが、哲学者ハンナ・アーレントが主張したように「悪というものは大罪人が行うのではなくて、ごく平凡な人間が何も自分で考えることなく、官僚的に処理するところから起きる」のかもしれません。アーレントは大学時代に映画『ハンナ・アーレント』（2012）で観るか書物で読んでみたいですね。肝に銘じたいことばです。

302

foreshadow

[fɔːrʃǽdou]

Verb   Literature

Def : to give a hint, sign or indication of something in advance

日 : 〜の前兆となる、〜の伏線となる

Syn : imply, signal, suggest

e. g. : In Dickens' works, spilled wine **foreshadows** spilled blood.（ディケンズの作品では、こぼれた葡萄酒がこぼれた血汐の前兆となっている）

Notes : Foreshadowing is a common literary technique that adds depth and complexity, and most of all suspense. 物語などで、後で起こる事をあらかじめほのめかしておくことを伏線といいます。

303

"Eureka!"

[juəríːkə]

Other   Conversation

Def : expressing joy on a discovery or insight

日 : わかった！これだ！（何かを発見した時の喜びを表す言葉）

Syn : I've got it! That's it!

e. g. : (Sigh) "I've no idea what to do. (Pause) **Eureka**! That's it!"（何をしたらいいものか、そうだ！それだ！）

Notes : I read this word today in a comic book. The character was confused and wondering what do and then he shouted to himself "Eureka!" Actually, in Japan there is a literary magazine called ユリイカ！ もともとはギリシア語に語源があります。そうか！

304

register

[rédʒəstər]

Noun   Linguistics

Def : the type of language used for a particular purpose or in a particular setting

日 : 言語使用域

Syn : NA

e. g. : "Please be quiet" and "Shut up" convey the same message in different **registers**.（「静かにしてください」と「うるさい」はメッセージは同じだがレジスターが違う）

Notes : Just as we dress differently for different occasions, we also use different styles of language depending on where we are and whom we are talking to. "Register" is the word used to refer to those differences. 場面によって英語を使い分けることも重要な英語コミュニケーション能力ですね。

（一口アドバイス）76　Why is it that giving guns is so easy but giving books is so hard? (Malala Yousafzai)

305

dismal

[dízm(ə)l]

Adjective　Conversation

Def : unpleasant, gloomy

日 : 陰気な、憂鬱な

Syn : dreary, dull, depressing

e.g. : "Our holiday was **dismal**. It rained every day and we all caught colds." (休暇は憂鬱だった。雨続きでおまけにみんな風邪を引いてしまった)

Notes : dismal は depressing, dull, cheerless の意味ですが、こういう形容詞をいくつも知っていると豊かな表現ができます。ちなみに、have a dismal face（憂鬱な顔をしている）などのようにも使われます。

306

horrendous

[hɔːréndəs]

Adjective　TOEIC

Def : extremely unpleasant, disturbing, or shocking

日 : 恐ろしい、法外な

Syn : fearful, dreadful, frightening

e.g. : The effects of the fire were **horrendous**. (火事による影響がおそろしかった)

Notes : It is a good word to know during the Halloween or when watching horror movies. ホラー映画の描写にどうぞ。

307

migration

[maɪgréɪʃ(ə)n]

Noun　Current

Def : the movement of animals or people from one country or place to live or work in another

日 : 仕事などの為に他の地域や国に移住すること

Syn : immigration / emigration

e.g. : **Migration** occurs for reasons such as for employment, quality of life, or survival. (移民は仕事、生活のため、生命の危機が理由に発生する)

Notes : Human migration from poorer countries or war zones to richer or safer countries is a fact of life in our world. But in those countries there is a lot of emotional debate about how much migration should be allowed and what kind of migrants to let in. 移民問題は地球上の全ての人にとって重要な問題です。

308

awareness

[əwéərnəs]

Noun　Academic

Def : feeling, experiencing or being conscious that something exists

日 : 気づいていること、認知度

Syn : perception, realization

e.g. : These days, there is more **awareness** of the LGBTQ society in Japan. (近年、日本では LGBTQ について の認知度が高まっている)

Notes : As you study in university, you become more aware of so many things outside your small community; things which you never thought had affected you in the past or what will seriously affect you in the future. 視野を広げる必要がありますね。

（一口アドバイス）77　Ask and it will be given to you; seek and you will find; knock and the door will be opened to you.

309   TCK (Third Culture Kid)

[θə́:r(d)_kʌ́ltʃər kíd]

Noun   Current

Def : children raised in a country other than their parents' home country

日 : 第三文化の子供たち

Syn : a transcultural child

e.g. : As a '**third culture kid**,' you live an interesting life, usually growing up in a country and culture different from that of your parents. (第三文化の子供として、君達は親とは異なる国や文化の中で成長し、楽しい人生を送るのだ)

Notes : More and more people not only live in more than one country during childhood but speak two or more languages and identify with various cultural values. Their identity is not tied to any one country or culture. TCK は世界を変えてゆくかもしれませんね。

---

310   mesmerize

[mézməràɪz]

Verb   Basic

Def : hold the attention of in a supernatural-like way

日 : 魅惑する、うっとりさせる

Syn : fascinate, hypnotize

e.g. : Juliet's angelic voice **mesmerized** the audience. (ジュリエットの美しい歌声に聴衆はうっとりとした)

Notes : mesmerize は、催眠療法を行ったオーストリア人医師 Franz Anton Mesmer（1734 − 1815）の名前に由来します。彼の治療法は "mesmerism"（メスメリズム）と呼ばれました。

---

311   research and development

[rɪsɔ́:rtʃ_ən dɪvélə(p)mənt]

Noun   TOEIC

Def : the act of researching and developing something

日 : 研究開発

Syn : R&D

e.g. : The Department of **Research and Development** was established to develop new drugs. (新薬開発のために研究開発部が設立された)

Notes : An R&D department in a company, one which requires creativity and critical thinking. 企業ではこのような部署が次々に設立され、新しい技術が生み出されています。

---

312   nonverbal communication

[nɑnvə́:rb(ə)l kəmjù:nəkéɪʃ(ə)n]

Noun   Communication

Def : the study of how we communicate without words, for example, using gestures, facial expressions, or touch

日 : ノンバーバルコミュニケーション

Syn : NA

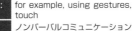

e.g. : In my **nonverbal communication** class, we studied eye contact, touch, personal space, and so on. (ノンバーバルコミュニケーションの授業ではアイコンタクトや接触、個人スペースについて学ぶ)

Notes : "Non-" is a prefix meaning "not" or "without," and "verbal"refers to words. When we think about communicating, we usually think about words, but a great part of our communication does not use words. コミュニケーションの大半は確かに言葉以外の要素でなされますね。

（一口アドバイス）78   If you're not making mistakes, then you're not doing anything. (John Wooden)

313 gender-neutral

[dʒéndər n(j)úːtrəl]

Adjective　Current

Def : referring to things such as clothing, personal behaviours, thoughts, emotions and/or relationships which are not regarded as either masculine nor feminine

日 : 性別による［男女の］区別のない

Syn : not regarded as either masculine or feminine

e.g. : That well-known clothing store in the city carries very **gender-neutral** fashion that are popular with both men and women. （あの有名なお店は男女の区別ないどちらにも人気の衣類をおいている）

Notes : This word describes the idea that society should avoid determining roles according to people's sex or gender, in order to avoid discrimination. 例文のようなお店も増えてきました。

314 apprehension

[æprɪhénʃ(ə)n]

Noun　Academic

Def : worry or strong concern about the future

日 : 不安、心配

Syn : anxiety

e.g. : It is normal to feel some **apprehension** before speaking in public. （人前で話す時に何かしらの不安を感じるのは普通のことだ）

Notes : To be "filled with apprehension" is a common phrase. また a feeling of apprehension で不安感という意味になります。

315 inbound

[ímbàund]

Adjective　Current

Def : towards the inside or centre of a place

日 : 入ってくる（外から国内へ）

Syn : inward

e.g. : Mie prefecture recorded the largest increase of **inbound** tourists this year. （三重県は今年最大の訪日外国人観光客の増加を記録した）

Notes : 外国からのという意味で単語として日本語の中でもこの inbound が使われることが多くなりました。the inbound train（大阪環状線のような内回り線）、an inbound bus（市内行きバス）のように内へ向かってというのが本来の意味です。

316 status quo

[stéɪtəs kwóu]

Noun　Basic

Def : current situation

日 : 現状

Syn : the current situation

e.g. : Steve Jobs stressed the importance of challenging the **status quo**. （スティーブ・ジョブズは現状に甘んぜず挑戦することの重要性を説いた）

Notes : quo はもともとラテン語ですが、challenge を伴って「現状に満足することなく挑戦する」というフレーズで覚えておくといいでしょう。大学生活だけでなく人生においても目の前の壁に挑戦を続けることは大切です。Challenge the status quo!

（一口アドバイス）79　学問とは真理をめぐる人間関係である。（松本紘）

317

exploit

[ɪksplɔ́ɪt]

Verb　　Basic

Def : treat someone unfairly in order to gain an advantage

日 : 搾取する

Syn : abuse, manipulate

e.g. : Even now a lot of children are **exploited** all over the world. （今も多くの子どもたちが世界中で搾取されている）

Notes : 英字新聞や Web の記事で目にすることの多い単語です。She exploited the situation to her advantage（彼女は状況を利用して自分の利益を図った）のように「使う」という意味でも使われます。

318

rhetorical question

[rɪtɔ́rɪk(ə)l kwéstʃ(ə)n]

Noun　　Communication

Def : a question asked for dramatic effect, not to gain information

日 : 答えを必要としない問いかけ

Syn : NA

e.g. : "How are you?" is often a **rhetorical question**. （How are you? は多くの場合、質問ではなくてレトリカル・クエスチョンだ）

Notes : Rhetorical questions are common in English and a good tool for the translator. "Saa"（さあ）in Japanese for example can be rendered "Who knows?" The implication is negative: "Nobody knows/ I don't know." 効果を上げるために使われる質問と本当に情報を問う質問を見分けたいですね

319

abuse

[əbjúːs]

Noun　　Basic

Def : spoken insults or physical violence

日 : 毒舌、虐待

Syn : insults, blame

e.g. : Cinderella's stepmother gave her a lot of **abuse**. （シンデレラは継母にこきおろされた）

Notes : abuse は child abuse（児童虐待）といったようにも使われます。名詞と動詞では発音が異なりますので注意しましょう。名詞は語末が /s/ の無声音、動詞は /z/ の有声音です。

320

dub

[dʌ́b]

Verb　　Communication

Def : replace spoken dialogue with dialogue in another language

日 : 吹き替える

Syn : NA

e.g. : US filmgoers generally prefer **dubbed** films to those with subtitles. （アメリカでは字幕付き映画より吹き替えのほうが人気があるようだ）

Notes : Most children's shows are dubbed, since children's reading skills aren't fully developed. It's harder to translate for dubbing since you have to pay attention to the actual movements of the character's lips and try to match them. ダビング（dubbing）は通常この説明のようにアフレコのことを言いますが、日本語でよく使う意味（CD などの複製）という意味もこのダビングにはあります。

（一口アドバイス）80　People are great because they are good.

321

merge

[mə́ːrdʒ]

Verb　　Basic

Def : join two or more things together

日 : 合併する

Syn : combine

e.g. : The two banks were **merged** to gain more profits. （二つの銀行は、利益を上げるために合併した）

Notes : 英語圏の国で車を運転する場合に、Merge という道路標識を見かけることがあります。これは、二つの道路や車線が一つになることを示しています。"mix," "mingle," "meld" 等、"m" で始まる同意語が多いのは偶然でしょうか。

322

aggressive

[əgrésɪv]

Adjective　　Basic

Def : behaving in an angry manner so that it appears you are likely to attack or confront someone

日 : 攻撃的な

Syn : hostile, quarrelsome, forceful.

e.g. : She is too **aggressive**. She tells people what to do and, if anyone has a different opinion, she gets angry and starts quarrelling. （彼女は攻撃的すぎる。指示ばかり出し、意見が違うと怒って喧嘩を始める）

Notes : 積極的と誤解されやすいですが、実際の意味はそれ以上です。例文のように攻撃的な意味を理解しましょう。積極的という意味の場合には、positive や active を使います（Her participation in the discussion was postive/active.）。

323

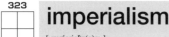

imperialism

[ɪmpíəriəlɪz(ə)m]

Noun　　Culture

Def : a political system in which one country has control over another

日 : 帝国主義

Syn : domination

e.g. : Japan has been criticized in the past by Korea and China for its history of **imperialism** in Asia. （日本はアジアにおける帝国主義の歴史から韓国と中国から批判されている）

Notes : Some poorer areas of the world still experience cultural imperialism in terms of the disappearance of their ethnic language and culture due to assimilation and/or acculturation. 帝国主義は昔のことではなく文化的帝国主義があることにも目を向けたいですね。

324

think outside (of) the box

[θɪŋk_âu(t)sàɪ(d)_ðə báks]

Other　　Current

Def : thinking differently, innovatively or creatively

日 : 創意工夫する

Syn : creative thinking

e.g. : We need to **think outside the box** to come up with something really unique and creative. （本当に何か他にない創造的なものを作りたかったら、発想を変える必要がある）

Notes : Students need to use creativity, critical thinking skills and imagination instead of continuing to learn under the conservative rules of past learning communities. Think outside the box! 発想を変えることは学問分野だけでなく人生において必要なことですね。　Think outside of the box と of を付けても OK です。

（一口アドバイス）81　Connect words to your heart, not just your head.

325 ethnocentric

[èθnouséntrik]

Adjective　Culture

Def : thinking that one's own group or culture is better or more important than others

日 : 自民族中心的な

Syn : anti-multicultural

e.g. : Thinking that only your culture is correct is just an **ethnocentric** viewpoint. It is too narrow. (自国の文化だけが正しいと思うことこそ自民族中心的な考え方だ。考え方が狭すぎるよ)

Notes : Thinking and behaving in an ethnocentric manner are quite natural and common for many people, but if we want to understand issues more broadly and communicate well with other nationalities, we need to move beyond an ethnocentric perspective. 広い視野が必要です。

---

326 linguistic pragmatics

[lɪŋgwístɪ(k)_prægmǽtɪks]

Noun　Linguistics

Def : the area of linguistics that deals with how language is used in social context, including politeness, taking turns, etc.

日 : 語用論 (丁寧表現など言語がいろいろな状況でどう使われるかについての研究)

Syn : NA

e.g. : When I studied **linguistic pragmatics**, I learned a lot about politeness. (語用論を学んだ際に、私は丁寧さについて多くの事を知った)

Notes : To use a language, you need to know more than the vocabulary and grammar. You need to understand how to use language in context -- that is linguistic pragmatics. 文脈の中での理解は本当に重要ですね。

---

327 perspective

[pərspéktɪv]

Noun　Basic

Def : the way people think about something, point of view

日 : 視点、観点

Syn : viewpoint

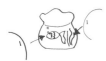

e.g. : We need to see the issue from a new **perspective**. (我々はその問題を新しい観点から見る必要がある)

Notes : 物事はいろいろな観点から見ないといけませんね。"different," "broader," "detached" などいろいろな形容詞を perspective の前につけて、文をつくってみましょう。

---

328 interlanguage

[íntərlæ̀ŋgwɪdʒ]

Noun　Linguistics

Def : the ability of a language learner to produce before they fully acquire the target language

日 : 中間言語

Syn : NA

e.g. : **Interlanguage** is a subject that is studied by some people who are interested in the learning of languages. (中間言語は言語学習に興味を持った人々によって研究されるトピックである)

Notes : "Inter" means "between." その他、例えば、international (国際的)、interaction (相互作用)、internet (インターネット) などがあります。Interlanguage はもともと造語です (Selinker, 1972)。

(一口アドバイス) 82　Dress up for your next position.

329 fulfill

[fulfil]

Verb　Basic

Def : complete (a task or an obligation)

日 : （約束を）果たす、実現させる

Syn : achieve

e. g. : Tadashi **fulfilled** his promise. （寔は約束を果たした）

Notes : "full" に "fill" が結合した合成語です。「満ち満ちた」感満載の語ですね。ちなみに、fullfill とスペルミスしがちなので気をつけてください。卒業論文の表紙で、This thesis is submitted in fulfillment of the requirements for the degree of Bachelor of English. と表記することがあります（名詞形は fulfillment ですが、イギリス英語では fulfilment と表記します。ややこしいですね）。

---

330 impartial

[ɪmpάːrʃ(ə)l]

Adjective　Basic

Def : unbiased, not showing any favour to anything over any other thing

日 : 偏見のない、公平な

Syn : fair, neutral, unbiased

e. g. : I want to be **impartial** in a group. （グループの中で中立な立場にいたい）

Notes : partial の「部分的」という意味だけ知っていたら「不完全」です。「とても好きな」「えこひいきする」という意味まであります。/p/ と /b/ の前に /n/ の音が来るときには、/n/ が /m/ になります（例えば、impossible, imbalance）。これは後続の音の準備を前の音でおこなう「同化」という音のきまりです。日本語の「てんぷら (tempura)」でも「ぷ」の前の「ん」は /m/ で発音されます。ただし、input, inpatient, inbound (No. 315) などの例外もありますので注意しましょう。

---

331 homonym

[hάːmənìm]

Noun　Linguistics

Def : words that have the same sound but different meanings

日 : 同音異義語

Syn : NA

e. g. : "Air" and "heir" are **homonyms** as are "there" and "their." （air [空気、エアー] と heir [相続人、エアー] は there [そこ、ゼア] と their [彼等の、ゼア] と同様に同音異義語だ）

Notes : "Homo" means "same," and "nym" means "name." また heterony（同形異音異義語）の例として、英語では lead（導く、鉛）、日本語では風車（かざぐるま＝おもちゃ、ふうしゃ＝水をくんだりする機械）があります。hetero は different という意味です。その他、pseudonym というと "pseudo"（偽の）で「偽名、ニックネーム」になります。

---

332 contamination

[kəntæ̀mənéɪʃ(ə)n]

Noun　Basic

Def : when dirt or other unpleasant materials are mixed with something pure

日 : 汚染

Syn : pollution

e. g. : There was a danger of **contamination** from nuclear waste. （核廃棄物からの汚染の危険があった）

Notes : Most often used relating to environmental damage. 環境問題を論じる際によく使われる単語です。

（一口アドバイス）83　When you are reading, don't stop to look new words up in a dictionary.

333

graceful

[gréɪsf(ə)l]

Adjective　Basic

Def : having simple, elegant beauty of form, manner, movement or speech

日 : 優雅な、上品は

Syn : elegant

e.g. : That dancer was so **graceful**. (あのダンサーはとっても優雅だ)

Notes : For describing beautiful movement or an elegant shape. 美しさの描写にどうぞ。

334

productive

[prədʌ́ktɪv]

Adjective　Linguistics

Def : creating a significant amount of something

日 : 産出的な、生産的な

Syn : constructive

e.g. : Speaking and writing are called **productive** skills. (スピーキングとライティングは産出的スキルである)

Notes : 語彙が多いということは、言語により表現することの可能性が拡がるということですね。そのためにも、a more productive environment（生産性の高い環境）をまわりに作り出すことが重要です。リスニングやリーディングは receptive skills（受容的なスキル）といわれます。

335

subordinate

[səbɔ́ːrd(ə)nət]

Noun　TOEIC

Def : a person who has a less important position than another person in an organization

日 : 部下

Syn : underling, junior

e.g. : The president of the company ordered her **subordinate** to find a place for the new branch. (社長は部下に支店の新しい候補地を探すように命令した)

Notes : ビジネスでよく使われる言葉です。

336

to distraction

[tu dɪstrǽkʃ(ə)n]

Other　Literature

Def : with mental distress

日 : 気が変になる程

Syn : madly

e.g. : "Oh, I love him **to** very **distraction** and misery and agony!" (わたしね、頭がヘンになりそうなくらい、苦しくって、息もできないくらい、あの人がすきなの！) (Hardy, 1874)

Notes : 例文のように、to distraction で気が変になりそうなくらい、という意味になります。この distraction は動転の意味ですが、こういう文脈で使えるのですね。また work without distraction（邪魔されずに集中して仕事をする）などのようにも使われます。

（一ロアドバイス）84　志を高く、挑戦して生きる。（平尾誠二）

337 blurred

[bláːrd]

Adjective   Literature

Def : unable to be seen clearly, out of focus

日 : ぼんやりした

Syn : dim

e.g. : "Is it Sergeant Troy?" said the **blurred** spot in the snow, tremulously. (「トロイ軍曹よね？」と雪の中の黒い点のようなぼやけた姿が震えた声で尋ねた) (Hardy, 1874)

Notes : blurred「ぼんやりした」という単語は、小説の中ではしょっちゅう出てきます。視界不良 (blurred vision)、ぼんやりとした記憶 (blurred memories)、ぼんやりとした境界線 (blurred boundary)、ぼやけた画像 (blurred image) など、私たちが何かを表現したい時にすぐに思いつく表現なのでしょうね。

338 elaborate

[ɪlǽbərèɪt]

Verb   Academic

Def : give further details or explanation

日 : 話などをさらに詳しく述べる

Syn : develop, expand

e.g. : Could you **elaborate** on your story? (もう少し詳しく述べてくれませんか？)

Notes : インタビューなどでよく使う言葉です。辞書には「精緻化」と書いてありますが、それでは意味がよく分からないですね。「詳しく述べて」「もう少し説明して下さい」という意味です。また elaborate <u>on</u> とセットで覚えておくと使いやすいです。日常会話でも使うことができる万能語。

339 suspense

[səspéns]

Noun   Literature

Def : excitement, tension or uncertainty about what may happen

日 : （結果がどうなるかわからない）宙ぶらりんの状態

Syn : tension

e.g. : The author skillfully prolonged the **suspense** till the climax. (作者はクライマックスまでハラハラドキドキ感を上手に引き延ばした)

Notes :「サスペンスドラマ」でおなじみのサスペンスですが、元来は、先がどうなるかわからなくて、読者をハラハラドキドキさせることをいいます。動詞形は suspend（保留する、停学にする）です。

340 messy

[mésɪ]

Adjective   Basic

Def : dirty or untidy, unkempt

日 : 汚い、散らかった

Syn : dirty

e.g. : Your room is too **messy**. Tidy up a bit. (あなたの部屋は汚すぎる。ちょっとは片付けなさい)

Notes : その他よく使われる表現として、My office is in a mess. などもあります。先生の研究室は概して散らかっていることが多いので、ボランティアで整理に行ってあげましょう。

（一口アドバイス）85　The most certain way to succeed is always to try just one more time. (Thomas Edison)

341

pat

[pǽt]

Verb　Basic

Def : touch something gently with the palm of an open hand

日 : 軽くたたく

Syn : tap

e.g. : My father **patted** me on the back. (父は優しく背中をポンとたたいた)

Notes : "slap"(「平手でぴしゃりと打つ」)、"tap"(「指先で軽くたたく」)など、触れ方にもいろいろあるのでまとめて覚えましょう。

342

"I got told off."

[aɪ gâ(t)_tòuld_ɑ́f]

Other　Conversation

Def : I was scolded (UK).

日 : 怒られた

Syn : I got yelled at.

e.g. : My mum found out that I lied. **I got** really **told off**. (母にウソがばれた。えらく怒られた)

Notes : 怒られた is a passive verb. "Got told off" is also passive, so it matches nicely. We use this expression in Britain a lot. "Got yelled at" is more common in America. 怒られたくはないですが、そのような状況を描写する際に。

343

in-text citation

[ɪntéks(t)_saɪtéɪʃ(ə)n]

Noun　Academic

Def : an academic convention that acknowledges the source of an idea when writing

日 : 引用（自分のレポートの中に他の本や論文を引用すること）

Syn : NA

e.g. : **In-text citations** are a key feature of academic writing. (引用はアカデミックライティングの重要な特徴だ)

Notes : In-text citations can be integral e.g. "Hada (2023) argues that…" or non-integral, "…" (Hada, 2023). アカデミックライティングで引用の方法を学ぶことは重要です。

344

alliteration

[əlìtəréɪʃ(ə)n]

Noun　Literature

Def : words that start with the same sound used consecutively or near each other

日 : 頭韻法（語頭の子音を同じまたは類似のものにする修辞技法）

Syn : NA

e.g. : President Bill Clinton said every child needs "a **h**appy **h**ome, a **h**ealthy family, and a **h**opeful future." (アメリカ大統領ビル・クリントンが演説の中で用いた頭韻法の例)

Notes : Alliteration appeals to the ear. It is useful in speeches as well as in writing. It shouldn't be overused, but it's a great tool to make words memorable. 確かに記憶に残りますね。

（一口アドバイス）86　Think different. (Steve Jobs)

345 legislation

[lèdʒəsléɪʃ(ə)n]

Noun　TOEIC

Def : a law or a set of laws

日 : 法律

Syn : law

e. g. : The current **legislation** does not take the gender gap into account. (現行の法律は性差を考慮していない)

Notes : law と legislation はよく似た意味ですが、law は可算名詞であるのに対し、legislation は不可算名詞です。

---

346 literal

[lít(ə)rəl]

Adjective　Communication

Def : having the same meaning as the original words

日 : 文字通り、逐語訳

Syn : word-for-word

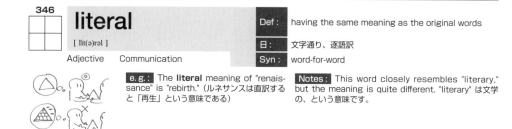

e. g. : The **literal** meaning of "renaissance" is "rebirth." (ルネサンスは直訳すると「再生」という意味である)

Notes : This word closely resembles "literary," but the meaning is quite different. "literary" は文学の、という意味です。

---

347 research question

[rɪsɔ́ːrtʃ kwéstʃ(ə)n]

Noun　Academic

Def : a question that identifies what will be studied

日 : 研究課題

Syn : NA

e. g. : What is your **research question**? (あなたはどのような研究をしていますか？)

Notes : 大学生の皆さんが遭遇するであろう会話。"What do you do?" "I'm a college student." "What's your major?" "Applied Linguistics." その次に、大抵、"What is your research question?"「何を研究しているのですか？」少くだいて言うなら「何に興味があるのですか？」卒論で、人生で、一番重要なのは、「何に取り組むか」ということかもしれません。そういう筆者は大学院生の時に世界的に著名な J.D. Brown 博士にこの質問をされたがこの言葉を知らなかったため、"What is your research question? What's that?" と質問してあきれられた苦い記憶があります。

---

348 infinite

[ínfənət]

Adjective　Basic

Def : unlimited, unending

日 : 無限の

Syn : limitless

e. g. : The problem with learning vocabulary is that the task seems **infinite**. (語彙学習の問題はキリがないことかもしれない)

Notes : Talking about distance or ability or love or … its uses are infinite! いろいろな場面に無限に活用できる単語です。発音（強勢）に気をつけましょう。前の音節に強勢がつきます。反意語は finite（限界のある）です。

（一口アドバイス）87　If winter comes, can spring be far behind? (Percy Shelley)

349

flirtatious

[fləːrtéɪʃəs]

Adjective　Conversation

Def : behaving as if you are attracted to someone, possibly without serious intentions

日 : 異性の気を引こうとする

Syn : playful, coquettish

e.g. : At a party it's fun to be a bit **flirtatious**. (パーティーでは少し異性の目を気にするのも楽しいものだ)

Notes : A little bit of flirting, being a bit flirtations, can be like adding spice to conversation: the spice of romance and of humor. 大人の世界ですね。

350

outlet

[áutlet]

Noun　Basic

Def : a device in a wall to which electronic equipment is connected to supply it with electricity

日 : コンセント

Syn : socket, power point

e.g. : Professor Kitao did not allow her students to connect their smartphones to the **outlet** in the classroom. (北尾教授は、生徒が教室でスマートフォンをコンセントに接続することを許さなかった)

Notes : コンセントは使用頻度の高い言葉ですが英語では outlet（主に北米）又は socket（主にイギリス）と言います。ホッチキスのように英語のようで日本語化されたものには注意したいですね。差し込む側のコード（電源プラグ）は plug と言います。国によってコンセントや電源プラグの形状や電圧が異なります。

351

symmetrical

[sɪmétrɪk(ə)l]

Adjective　Current

Def : having parts that match each other exactly, for example a mirror image

日 : 対称な

Syn : balanced

e.g. : The Taj Mahal in India is perfectly **symmetrical**. (インドのタージマハルは完全対称の建物だ)

Notes : Great word for talking about art, design and apppearances. シンメトリカルとして日本語でも使われることが多くありますね。特に建築やアートでは頻出の単語です。

352

sizzling

[síz(ə)lɪŋ]

Adjective　Basic

Def : very hot

日 : ジュージューと音を立てている（熱い）

Syn : sweltering （天気）　　piping hot （食べ物）

e.g. : The dish was topped with a **sizzling** hot fried egg. （料理の上に熱々の目玉焼きがのっていた）

Notes : A good word to use to make your writing or speaking more vivid. sizzling steak というとジュージューと音が聞こえてきそうな熱々のステーキ。その他、sizzling summer（うだるように暑い夏）などともいうことができます。

（一口アドバイス）88　If you're going to do it, do it.

353 erode

[ɪróud]

Verb　Academic

Def : wear away over a long period of time

日 : 浸食する

Syn : wear away

e.g.: Unfortunately severe flood waters last year **eroded** the banks of the Kamo River.（昨年の洪水のため鴨川の堤防が浸食された）

Notes : TOEFL などでよく出てくる単語です。このような一語が分からないと全体が何を言っているのか分からなくて困ることもあります。併せて erosion（浸食）も覚えておきましょう。

---

354 incessant

[ɪnsés(ə)nt]

Adjective　Basic

Def : never stopping, ceaseless

日 : 絶え間ない

Syn : continuous

e.g.: Due to **incessant** heavy rains, the baseball game was cancelled.（絶え間ない豪雨のために、その野球の試合は中止になった）

Notes : 副詞形の "incessantly"（絶え間なく）もよく使われるので、一緒に覚えておきましょう。

---

355 relocation

[r̀ːloukéɪʃ(ə)n]

Noun　TOEIC

Def : the movement of people or things to a new place

日 : 移転

Syn : transfer, resettlement

e.g.: The **relocation** site has yet to be decided.（移転先はまだ決定していない）

Notes : Used when describing historical facts about communities that were forced out of their homes to move somewhere else. 歴史的にも使われますが、例えば capital relocation（首都移転）や基地などの relocation plan（移転計画）などにも使われます。

---

356 contingency

[kəntíndʒ(ə)nsɪ]

Noun　Literature

Def : possible future event that cannot be predicted

日 : 不測の事態、思わぬ出来事

Syn : emergency, accident

e.g.: You knew what married life would be like, and shouldn't have entered it if you feared these **contingencies**.（結婚生活がこんなものだって、わかっていたはずだ。こんな思いがけない出来事をいちいち懸念しているんじゃ、はじめから結婚なんか、しなけりゃよかったんだ）(Hardy, 1874)

Notes : イギリスの作家ハーディの好きな単語です。偶然、偶発、不慮の出来事は、ハーディの人生観にも通じるテーマです。ちなみに、contingency table というとクロス集計表。統計学の授業で教授が何度もこの言葉を使っていましたが、contingency の「緊急の、偶発の」という意味からつながらなくて最初ピンとこなかったのを思い出します。

（一口アドバイス）89　Don't go through life, grow through life. (Eric Butterworth)

357 metaphorical

[mètəfɔ́:rɪk(ə)l]

Adjective　　Literature

Def : not literal; a figure of speech

日 : 隠喩的な

Syn : figurative

e.g. : "Salad bowl" is a common **metaphorical** description of the United States. (アメリカ合衆国のことをたとえていうとき、「サラダ・ボウル」、つまり「多民族の共生」という表現がよく使われる)

Notes : This word forms a contrasting pair with "literal." (No. 346) "Melting pot" has also been used as a metaphor for American society, where many different kinds of people blend together and become Americanized. 日本語でもメタファーと言われますね。

---

358 cognate

[kά:gneɪt]

Noun　　Linguistics

Def : words that share the same origin

日 : 同語源の言葉

Syn : NA

e.g. : 'Jahr' in German is a **cognate** with 'year' in English. (ドイツ語のJahrは英語のyearと語源が同じだ)

Notes : 英語やドイツ語はインドヨーロッパ語族 (language family) に属します。その関係で語源を同一とする言葉が異なる言語 (英語、ドイツ語、フランス語など) に存在します。例えば、ゼミという seminar は三言語で同じ綴りです。ちなみにゼミというのはドイツ語 (ゼミナール) から来ています。

---

359 denote

[dɪnóut]

Verb　　Linguistics

Def : represent or symbolize

日 : 表示する、〜の印である

Syn : show

e.g. : On a map, there is a special symbol that **denotes** a post office. (地図には郵便局を示す特別の記号がある)

Notes : Contrast "denote" with "connotation." Denote shows a direct relationship between the symbol and its meaning. A connotation is less obvious, but a strong relationship may still exist. denote では明示するという意味合いですね。

---

360 green fingers

[grí:n fíŋgərz]

Noun　　Current

Def : being good at making plants grow well or gardening

日 : 園芸の才

Syn : be a good gardener

e.g. : Her garden always looks wonderful. She has **green fingers**. (彼女の庭はいつも素晴らしい。園芸の才能がありますね)

Notes : 同じ意味で "He has a green thumb." とも言います。アメリカでは一般的な表現です。thumb は親指という意味。

(一口アドバイス) 90　Every artist was first an amateur. (Ralph Emerson)

361 expendable

[ɪkspéndəb(ə)l]

Adjective　Basic

Def : not essential, to be discarded after use

日 : 消耗品の

Syn : disposable

e. g. : I don't want to spend a lot of money on **expendable** office supplies. (消耗品である事務用品に多くのお金を使いたくない)

Notes : 受験生時代に"expensive expendable office supplies"という組み合わせで覚えた単語です。無駄にお金を使いたくはないが、高価な消耗品の中には、「さすが」と思わざるを得ない、いいものもありますね。

---

362 social media

[sóuʃəl míːdiə]

Noun　Communication

Def : types of digital communication platforms that allow people to share information via the internet

日 : ソーシャルメディア

Syn : SNS

e. g. : News of the terrorist attack spread rapidly on **social media**. (テロの情報がソーシャルメディアによってまたたく間に広がった)

Notes : Although "SNS" is used in Japan and other countries, overseas "social media" is used. 欧米では social media、日本などでは SNS がよく使われます。

---

363 devastate

[dévəstèɪt]

Verb　TOEIC

Def : destroy or damage very badly

日 : 壊滅させる

Syn : destroy

e. g. : Kobe City was **devastated** by the earthquake in 1995. (1995年の阪神淡路大震災によって神戸市は壊滅的な被害をうけた)

Notes : This word can also be used metaphorically to show that someone is very upset by a situation. 例えば、She was devastated by her lost love.「失恋の痛手は大きい」などのように。

---

364 consecutive

[kənsék(j)ətɪv]

Adjective　TOEIC

Def : following one thing after another without interruption

日 : 連続した

Syn : continuous, sequential, successive

B567AAA2CX

e. g. : I had three **consecutive** holidays. (三連休でした)

Notes : スポーツなどで、third consecutive victory というと三連勝となります。An advanced level of vocabulary to use professionally or academically.

(一口アドバイス) 91　Be kind, for everyone you meet is fighting a hard battle.

365

corpus linguistics

[kɔ́ːrpəs lɪŋgwístɪks]

Noun　　Linguistics

Def : the study of language, based on a collection of texts, sometimes made up of hundreds of millions or billions of words

日 : コーパス言語学

Syn : NA

e.g. : I study **corpus linguistics** to understand what words are often used together. (どの単語と単語が一緒に使われるかを理解するのにコーパス言語学は役に立ちます)

Notes : You can search a corpus, (such as one at https://www.english-corpora.org) to understand how particular words are used in context. 実際にこの Web page をご覧下さい。

366

lucid

[lúːsəd]

Adjective　　Academic

Def : clearly expressed and easy to understand, logical

日 : 明快な

Syn : crystal clear

e.g. : Professor Tsuji gave a **lucid** explanation on that issue. (辻教授はその問題について明快な説明をおこなった)

Notes : 接頭辞や接尾辞から類推することのできないこのような単語は覚えておくに尽きます。

367

pagan

[péɪgən]

Adjective　　Literature

Def : belonging to one of the belief systems that existed before the main world religions

日 : 異教の

Syn : heathen

e.g. : Both Christmas and Easter are originally **pagan** festivals. (クリスマスとイースターはどちらも、もともと異教の祭りだった)

Notes : クリスマスもイースターも、もともとは古代ケルト人の祭りでした。

368

integrity

[ɪntégrəti]

Noun　　TOEIC

Def : the awareness of and ability to do what is morally right

日 : 正直さ、完全さ

Syn : virtue

no lie for life.

e.g. : Her personal **integrity** was respected by all who knew her. (彼女の誠実な人柄が皆の尊敬を集めた)

Notes : "integr-"（「完全な」）を接頭辞に持つ単語（"integral," "integrate" 等）も併せて覚えましょう。

（一口アドバイス）92　Read, and then read, and then read some more.

pragmatic

[prægmǽtɪk]

Adjective　Current

Def : doing what people think is best, or most effective, disregarding theoretical concerns

日 : 現実的な

Syn : practical

e.g. : Professor Susser usually took a **pragmatic** approach to curriculum reform of the English department. (サッサー教授は英語英文学科のカリキュラム改訂にはいつも現実的手法を取った)

Notes : 反対語（antonym）は unrealistic、impractical です。ものごとの解決には時に現実的な手法を取ることが必要ですね。

---

alleged

[əlédʒ(ə)d]

Adjective　Academic

Def : said or thought by some people, whether or not there is evidence to support it

日 : そうおもわれている、疑惑のある

Syn : supposed, unproven

e.g. : Area 51 is famous for being an **alleged** alien landing spot. (エリア51はエイリアンが着陸した疑惑の場所として有名だ)

Notes : ニュースを聞いていて必ず出てくる用語です。allege は動詞では主張する、過去分詞で形容詞的に使われると「主張された」→「疑いのある」という意味になります。当然犯罪関係が多くなります。alleged assault（暴行容疑）、alleged affair（不倫疑惑）、見たくない言葉ばかりですが印象には残りますね。

---

volatile

[vɑ́:lət(ə)l]

Adjective　TOEIC

Def : likely to change suddenly

日 : 変動しやすい

Syn : unstable

e.g. : Recently, we have been seeing increasingly **volatile** weather patterns in Kyoto. （最近、京都の天気は不安定なパターンが多い）

Notes : 海外のニュースでこの言葉がよく使われるのは、天気と為替、volatile currency（不安定な通貨）など。

---

rationale

[ræ̀ʃənǽl]

Noun　Academic

Def : the reasons for something; a plan of action

日 : 理由

Syn : reason (s), grounds

e.g. : This chapter presents the **rationale** for this study. (この章ではこの研究をする理由を述べる)

Notes : 卒論で一番重要なのは研究する動機。その理由を rationale といいます。理論的な背景（theoretical rationale）も重要ですが個人的な理由（personal rationale）が研究を突き動かします。研究の背景には個人の経験があるのです。形容詞形は rational（合理的）と e を抜いた形になります。

（一口アドバイス）93　突破！突破！すべてに現状を突破して、一路向上すべし。（出口日出麿）

373

neurotic

[n(j)uərάːtɪk]

Adjective　Conversation

Def : overly anxious, or nervous about something that does not justify such concern

日 : 神経病的な

Syn : obsessive, anxious

e. g. : You cannot relax at his place, 'cause it's always super-clean! He's so **neurotic**. (あいつの家に行っても、いつもピカピカ過ぎてリラックスできないよ！あいつ、あれこれ神経質すぎるんだよな)

Notes : 語の元の意味は…省略しますが、精神分析学の祖フロイトの用語に由来する由緒正しい（？）スラングです。使いどころが難しいですが、友人同士の会話にうまく入れたりすると笑いがとれるでしょう。

374

interpersonal communication

[ˌɪntərpˈɚːrs(ə)n(ə)l kəmjùːnəkéɪʃ(ə)n]

Noun　Communication

Def : the study of communication in social relationships

日 : 対人コミュニケーション

Syn : NA

e. g. : Studying **interpersonal communication** has helped me understand how to have better relationships with my friends. (対人コミュニケーションを学ぶことによって友達と良き関係の築き方を理解することができた)

Notes : "Inter" means "between." その他、例えば、international（国際的）、interaction（相互作用）、internet（インターネット）などがあります。対人コミュニケーションではジェスチャーなどのノンバーバルコミュニケーション（No. 312）は重要な研究テーマです。特にハグや握手など人と人の接触を扱う学問領域を haptics（接触についての研究、触覚学）と言います。

375

congruence

[kάːŋgruəns]

Noun　Academic

Def : the state of agreeing or corresponding

日 : 一致

Syn : harmony

e. g. : When several experiments get the same results, this is an example of **congruence**. (いくつかの実験で同じ結果が出た時などが、この単語の意味を表すよい例となる)

Notes : The adjectival form of this word can be used in many situations e.g."A is congruent with B" 例 え ば、The reputation of the English department is congruent with the reality. (英語英文学科の評判は現実の姿と一致します) のように使うことができます。

376

pension

[pénʃ(ə)n]

Noun　Current

Def : money paid regularly to someone who is old or retired

日 : 年金、恩給

Syn : welfare payment

e. g. : We are living on a **pension**. (私たちは年金暮らしだ)

Notes : 日本語では軽井沢のペンションなどという時に使われますが、英語では通常 pension は年金、恩給を指します。食事付きの小さなホテルを pension と言っても間違いではありませんが（もともとフランス語）、英語では resort inn の方が一般的でしょう。

(一口アドバイス) 94　If you don't step forward, you're always in the same place. (Nora Roberts)

377 collectivism

[kəléktıvìzm]

Noun   Communication

Def : the belief that the needs of the country or group are more important than those of the individual

日 : 集産主義

Syn : NA

e.g. : One of the characteristics of Japanese culture lies in **collectivism**. (日本文化の特徴の一つに集産主義がある)

Notes : Collectivism の日本語訳は集産主義ですが集団主義と考えても間違いではありません。ところで、個人主義 (individualism) と対比して集団主義と言われますが、groupism ではなくて正確には collectivism を使います。日本社会・文化の特徴としてよく使われる表現なので覚えておきたいですね。その他、日本文化の特徴は masculinity（男性社会）⇄女性社会（femininity）という言葉でも表されます。

---

378 subsidy

[sʌ́bsədi]

Noun   TOEIC

Def : money given (often by a governing body) as part of the cost of something

日 : 補助金

Syn : aid

e.g. : The Japanese government gives a **subsidy** to promote research on English education for high school. (日本政府は高校の英語教育を向上させるための研究に補助金を交付している)

Notes : 人はひとりでは生きていけないのと同様に、研究や事業にもいろいろな機関からのサポートをしてもらうことが必要になることがあります。強勢は前にあります。関連する語に subsidize（動詞；補助金を出す）、subsidiary（子会社）があります。ビジネス文書でよく使う単語です。

---

379 personification

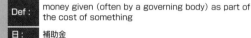

[pərsὰnəfəkéıʃ(ə)n]

Noun   Literature

Def : assigning human traits to something

日 : 擬人法

Syn : representing as a person

e.g. : An example of **personification** is "My computer doesn't like me." (「PCは私を嫌っている」などが擬人法の例)

Notes : Personification is a literary technique, but it's also used in everyday speech, as the example shows. 文学だけでなく、日常生活でも有効な方法ですね。

---

380 F-word

[éfwə̀:rd]

Noun   Communication

Def : a way to refer to the offensive word "fuck" without actually using it

日 : F で始まる汚い言葉

Syn : NA

e.g. : Kids these days use swear words like the **F-word** without a second thought. (最近の子供は何の考えもなしに F-word を使う)

Notes : いわゆる "four letter words" の代表 "fuck"。学校では習いませんが、日常・メディア至るところに溢れています。それを口にするのをはばかられる場面で使うのが、"F-word"。「黒人」を表す差別語を表現する時に使う "N-word" もあります。ただし、表記するときは F*** とし、F-word とは書きません。

(一口アドバイス) 95 Don't stop believing. (Glee, Journey)

381

seclusion

[sɪklúːʒ(ə)n]

Noun   TOEIC

Def : the state of being alone, in privacy

日 : 隔絶

Syn : isolation

e. g. : Many college students spent a week in **seclusion**, preparing for the final exam. (大学生の多くは最終テストのために1週間家に引きこもって勉強した)

Notes : その他、national seclusion（江戸時代の鎖国）という形でも使うことができます。

382

impersonate

[ɪmpə́ːrs(ə)nèɪt]

Verb   Literature

Def : pretend to be someone else

日 : ～の役を演じる、真似る

Syn : imitate, mimic

e. g. : Hiroshi became well-known for **impersonating** the president. (宏は大統領のものまねで一世を風靡した)

Notes : "impersonate" は演劇を語るときには外せない用語です。歌舞伎の「女形（おやま）」は "female impersonator" です。

383

concession

[kənséʃ(ə)n]

Noun   Academic

Def : something that is given up or offered to another party in order to end a disagreement

日 : 譲歩

Syn : compromise

e. g. : The firm will be forced to make **concessions** to the union. (その会社は組合に譲歩せざるを得なかった)

Notes : Often seen in political news e.g. "The government refuses to make concessions to the terrorists." 政治ニュースでも使われる単語ですね。

384

derogatory

[dɪrɑ́ːgətɔ̀ːri]

Adjective   Communication

Def : expressing a negative opinion of someone or something

日 : 軽蔑的な

Syn : belittling, degrading

e. g. : The politician made **derogatory** statements about women. (あの政治家が女性に対する軽蔑的な発言をした)

Notes : Learners of English (as well as learners of other languages) need to be careful in choosing words when expressing themselves to avoid something discriminatory. 適切な言葉の使い方は大切です。

（一口アドバイス）96 Opposition is true friendship. (William Blake)

385 suffix

[sʌ́fɪks]

Noun　Linguistics

Def : a word part that is added to the end of a word, for example -ing, -able, etc.

日 : 接尾辞

Syn : NA

e.g. : **Suffixes** often change words from one part of speech to another. (接尾辞によって単語の品詞が変わることが多い)

Notes : The suffix "-ly" can change an adjective (cold) into an adverb (coldly). 例えば、ly をつけることによって形容詞が副詞になります。

386 complex

[kɑ́:mplèks]

Noun　Basic

Def : an unhealthy and powerful feeling (e.g. that you are worse than others)

日 : 強迫観念

Syn : neurosis

e.g. : She has an inferiority **complex** about her looks. (彼女は自分の容姿に劣等感をいだいている)

Notes : コンプレックス＝劣等感と思われがちだが、劣等感は "inferiority complex" が正しい表現です。形容詞としては「複雑な」という意味がある。

387 proliferate

[prəlíf(ə)rèɪt]

Verb　Academic

Def : increase dramatically and suddenly in number

日 : 急増する

Syn : increase

e.g. : Research on early childhood education has **proliferated** in Japan over the last decade. (日本ではここ 10 年で早期英語教育についての研究が激増した)

Notes : 論文など adademic writing でよく見かける単語です。レポートなどで使ってみたいですね。

388 versatile

[vɔ́:rsət(ə)l]

Adjective　Basic

Def : able to do many different things

日 : 多用途の、融通が利く、多才な

Syn : having many different uses

e.g. : Professor Takayama was **versatile**, able to teach various kinds of courses. (高山教授は何でもこなせる人で、様々な科目を教えることができた)

Notes : DVD ディスクはよく目にするメディアですが、Digital Versatile Disc（デジタル多用途ディスク）の略です。

（一口アドバイス）97　Plan your work, work your plan. (John Wooden)

389

commitment

[kəmí(t)mənt]

Noun　Academic

Def : willingness to give your time, energy or money to something

日 : 献身、深い関与

Syn : dedication

e.g.: I respect my colleagues who have **commitment** to their work.（仕事に打ちこんでいる同僚には敬意を払う）

Notes : 政治家の公約や委託の意味で覚えることが多いかもしれませんが、例文のように、何かに対する献身や傾倒といった意味でも使うことが多い単語です。

390

unbearable

[ʌnbéərəb(ə)l]

Adjective　Conversation

Def : too painful or unpleasant

日 : 我慢できない

Syn : unendurable

e.g.: The situation was **unbearable** and I had to leave.（耐えがたい状況だったので、私は立ち去らざるを得なかった）

Notes : 「もう我慢ならない」と言う際に、"I can't stand it." とか "I can't endure this." といいますが、その変わりに使う形容詞です。

391

ambience

[ǽmbiəns]

Noun　Literature

Def : the character, atmosphere or mood of a place

日 : （ある）場所の雰囲気

Syn : atmosphere

e.g.: The customers enjoyed the refined **ambience** of the hotel.（顧客はそのホテルの洗練された雰囲気を楽しんだ）

Notes : 「雰囲気」を意味する言葉は他にも "mood," "vibe," "aura" などがあります。用例を確かめて使いこなしましょう。

392

etymology

[ètəmáːlədʒi]

Noun　Linguistics

Def : the explanation of the origins of a word

日 : 語源学

Syn : origin

e.g.: Understanding the **etymology** of a word is useful.（言葉の語源を知ることはとても役に立つ）

Notes : Understanding the etymology of a word helps to connect it to other words with related meanings. 語源を知ることによって単語も覚えやすくなります。

（一口アドバイス）98　良い聴き手になることは雄弁よりもむずかしい。

mediated communication

[míːdièɪtɪ(d)_kəmjùːnəkéɪʃ(ə)n]

Noun   Communication

Def : communication through a mechanical device, such as a telephone or a computer

日 : コンピュータなどの媒体を通したコミュニケーション

Syn : NA

e.g. : **Mediated communication** allows me to keep in touch with my friends in other countries. (媒介コミュニケーションによって他の国や地域に住む友人と連絡を取ることができる)

Notes : Mediated communication, particularly computer mediated communication, has become a larger and larger part of our communication. E-mail や SNS などもこのコミュニケーションの形態ですね。CMC (computer mediated communication) とも略されます。

394

intercultural competence

[ˌɪntərkʌ́ltʃ(ə)rəl kɑ́ːmpət(ə)ns]

Noun   Communication

Def : the ability to effectively communicate in an appropriate way with people of other cultures

日 : 異文化間コミュニケーション能力

Syn : intercultural ability

e.g. : Students can improve their **intercultural competence** by studying abroad and communicating with people from various ethnic and social backgrounds (異文化間コミュニケーション能力は留学や多様な民族・社会的背景の人達と交流することにより伸長できる)

Notes : In some ways, improving one's intercultural competence is more important than improving one's English ability, in order to communicate with people from different cultures. コミュニケーション能力に必要不可欠なものですね。

395

condemn

[kəndém]

Verb   Academic

Def : state very strongly that something is very bad

日 : とがめる、非難する

Syn : criticize

e.g. : The bad behaviour of the students was **condemned** by the teacher. (先生は学生たちの行儀悪さをとがめた)

Notes : Another 'political news' word, e.g. "The actions of the government were condemned by the public." 政治ニュースでも使われる単語ですね。

396

affluent

[ǽfluənt]

Adjective   Academic

Def : rich

日 : 豊か

Syn : wealthy

e.g. : Keisuke was born in an **affluent** household. (敬介は裕福な家庭に生まれた)

Notes : an advanced level of vocabulary to use professionally or academically. エッセイなどで使ってみたいですね。

（一口アドバイス）99 Gather ye rosebuds while ye may. (Robert Herrick)

397

filthy

[fílθi]

Adjective　Basic

Def : very dirty (for concrete objects or also someone's disgusting behaviour or language)

日 : 不潔な、下品な、機嫌の悪い

Syn : mucky, soiled, dirty

e. g. : The river is **filthy**. (その川はとても汚い)

Notes : When I was living in a dorm in the U.S, I learned this word. 実際の会話で使われる単語ですね。

398

run in the family

[rʌ́n_ɪn ðə fǽm(ə)li]

Phrase　Conversation

Grandpa　Dad　New me

Def : used to show that family members share the same characteristics

日 : 代々…の血筋である、遺伝する

Syn : an inherited trait; "Like father, like son"

e. g. : What a wonderfully inventive work of art! She's quite an artist. Does it **run in the family**? (素晴らしい芸術作品ですね。彼女はなかなかの芸術家だ。代々その血筋なの?)

Notes : "It skips a generation." で「隔世遺伝だ」という意味になる。「世代を一つ越えた遺伝」と表現するのがおもしろいですね。

399

infatuated

[ɪnfǽtʃuèɪtɪd]

Adjective　Conversation

Def : feelng intense but short-lived passion or attraction

日 : 夢中になって、のぼせ上がって

Syn : charmed

e. g. : The girl was **infatuated** with the actor who played Romeo. (その少女はロミオ役の俳優に夢中になった)

Notes : 「何かに心を奪われる」という表現は、外からの力によって動かされる状態を表すので、受動態になることが多いですね。infatuate（夢中にさせる）もあわせて覚えておきましょう。

400

virtuous circle

[vɚ́ːrtʃuə(s)_sɚ́ːk(ə)l]

Other　Academic

Def : a continuing cycle of events, each one increasing the beneficial power of the next

日 : 正の連鎖

Syn : a good cycle

e. g. : To create a **virtuous circle** in English learning, start by learning vocabulary. (英語学習の好循環を生み出すには語彙学習から始めることだ)

Notes : 反対の vicious circle（負の連鎖）はよく知っているのに、なぜか反対の好循環を知らないという人は多いのでは。人生で正の連鎖を生むヒントを探したいものですね。なお、vicious/virtuous cycle ともいう。

（一口アドバイス）100　When one door closes, another opens. (Graham Bell)

付録：日本人英語学習者がよく間違える英語30

NO	Key words	誤用例	→	訂正例	説明
1	all student	All <u>student</u> had to attend the class.	→	All **students** had to attend the class.	複数にするべき名詞が単数のままになっているミス。多くの学生に見られる。
2	almost	<u>Almost</u> Japanese people like rice.	→	**Most** Japanese people like rice. **Almost all** Japanese people like rice.	学生は "most" の代わりによく "almost" を使いますが間違いです。代わりに "most" または "almost all" を使いましょう。
3	And	This week, I learned about verbal phrases. <u>And</u> I learned about some useful idioms.	→	This week, I learned about verbal phrases. **In addition,** I learned about some useful idioms.	文法的に間違っているわけではありませんが、アカデミックライティングでは、"And" で文を始めないようにしましょう。
4	at first	<u>At first,</u> I will explain what I did during the weekend.	→	**First,** I will explain what I did during the weekend.	at first と first の混同
5	Because	<u>Because</u> I could not submit the homework.	→	I was disappointed in myself **because** I could not submit the homework.	従属節のみで文を終えてはいけない。
6	besides	I have a beautiful sofa <u>besides</u> the table.	→	I have a beautiful sofa **beside** the table.	beside と besides は、意味が異なる。
7	But	Cooking is very difficult for me. <u>But,</u> the more I practice, the more I can improve.	→	Cooking is very difficult for me. **However,** the more I practice, the more I can improve.	文法的に間違っているわけではありませんが、アカデミックライティングでは、"But" で文を始めないようにしましょう。
8	challenge	I <u>challenged to</u> write a good paragraph.	→	I **tried to** write a good paragraph.	英語の challenge には「試合、決闘に挑む」という意味が強いので、try を使いましょう。
9	could	I <u>could</u> make a lot of friends.	→	I **made** a lot of friends. I **was able to** make a lot of friends.	could は「しようと思えばできる」という意味になるので、「〜できた」を英語にする場合は動詞の過去形を用いるか "be able to" を用いること。

NO	Key words	誤用例	→	訂正例	説明
10	discuss	We need to discuss <u>about</u> this problem.	→	We need to **discuss** this problem.	discuss の使い方。この問題について話し合う必要がある、という場合に、about を入れてしまう。
11	driver's license	I went to Tottori with my friend to get <u>driver's license.</u>	→	I went to Tottori with my friend to get **a** <u>driver's license.</u>	冠詞 (a) が抜けやすいです。
12	each other	Our group members talked <u>each other.</u>	→	Our group members talked **to** each other.	前置詞がもれていますよ。
13	easy	<u>I was easy to under-stand</u> the lesson.	→	**It** was **easy for** me **to** understand the lesson.	I was easy to under-stand. は OK. でも「私は（他の人にとって）分かりやすい」という意味
14	enjoy	I <u>was very enjoy.</u>	→	I **enjoyed myself** yesterday.	品詞が誤っている。enjoy は他動詞、目的語も必要 (Enjoy! と言うことは OK)
15	get used to	I <u>am getting used to discuss</u> the issue with classmates.	→	I am **getting used to discussing** the issue with classmates.	不定詞の to か前置詞の to かの判別
16	graduate	I <u>graduated</u> high school.	→	I <u>graduated</u> **from** high school.	前置詞 from を付加せず使わないように、セットで覚えよう。
17	had better	You <u>had better</u> buy crackers for the deer in Nara.	→	You **should** buy crackers for the deer in Nara.	"had better" は厳しいアドバイスになります。"should" "could" "why don't you…?" が適切です。
18	have written	She <u>have written 10</u> pages of this book.	→	She **has** written **ten** pages of this book.	3人称単数現在の -s はよく間違えます。見直しましょう。
19	homework	I had so <u>many home-work</u> yesterday.	→	I had so **much** home-work (many **assign-ments**) yesterday.	homework は集合名詞なので数えません。数える場合には assignment を
20	I think	I <u>think I want to</u> study hard.	→	I **want to** study hard.	「〜したいと思う」を英語にする時は "I think" は不要。"want to" だけで「したいと思う」という意味

NO	Key words	誤用例	→	訂正例	説明
21	In this week	In this week, I have to practice typing a lot.	→	**This week**, I have to practice typing a lot.	this week に in を付けてしまうミス
22	live	I am going to a live.	→	I am going to a **gig (concert, performance)**.	ライブではなくて concert (classical music) 又は gig (popular music)
23	look forward to	I'm looking forward to see you in the US.	→	I'm **looking forward to seeing** you in the US.	前置詞の to のパターンです。
24	more than	The film moved me than I first expected.	→	The film moved me **more than** I first expected.	比較級を使った不完全な文章になってしまっています。
25	my friend	Today class I checked syllabus and we talked with my friend about the summer vacation.	→	**In** today's class, **we (I)** checked **the** syllabus and talked with **our (my) friends** about the summer vacation.	I と we の混合は不要ですね。もしするなら my friend → our friends に
26	play	I'll play with my friends tomorrow.	→	I'll **hang out with** my friends tomorrow.	play with は子どもの場合に使う表現なので、大学生の場合は hang out with
27	problems	I found difficult to answer the listening problems.	→	I found **it** difficult to answer the listening **questions**.	「問題」はすべて problem ではありません。
28	read	During the summer vacation, I readed two novels that the professor recommended.	→	During the summer vacation, I **read** two novels that the professor recommended.	不規則動詞の正しい活用形、発音でも [ri:d-red-red] と発音することにも注意
29	score	My TOEIC score was good score.	→	My TOEIC score was **good**.	同じ語を無駄に繰り返さないように
30	visited	When I was a child, I have visited the Zoo very often.	→	When I was a child, I **visited** the Zoo very often.	「行ったことがある（経験）」から現在完了を使おうとしているのでしょうが、過去形と、現在完了形は同時に使えない。

このリストは同志社女子大学英語英文学科における 2020〜2023 年度までの学科プロジェクト ELJ (English Learning Journal) をもとに分析したものです。

索　引

執筆者一覧 (14名、ABC順)

Juliet W. Carpenter, David Clayton，今井由美子，S. Kathleen Kitao，
風間末起子，甲元洋子，小山薫，松村延昭，Timothy L. Medlock，湊圭史，
Michi Ann Saki，玉田佳子，辻英子，若本夏美

イラスト
永井花連，中山美織，東玲那，大谷彩香，山田愛与，今井茉梨乃

表紙（原案）
東玲那

音声
Michi Ann Saki

協力
英語英文学科学生 2016 年度在籍生 695 名
城戸葵，森西光（文学研究科大学院生）
浮網佳苗，Joanna Caroline Grote，木島菜菜子，山本由実（英語英文学科）
余田由香利，粟津永子，尼川佐知子（英語英文学会事務局）
狩野裕也（明文舎印刷）

編集委員会（ABC順）
福島祥一郎，今井由美子，Michi Ann Saki，鈴木健司，若本夏美（代表）

（敬称略）

同志社女子大学英語英文学会
(The English Society of Doshisha Women's College of Liberal Arts)
1967 年に設立。同志社女子大学表象文化学部（2008 年まで学芸学部）英語英文学科、大学院文学研究科英語英文学専攻の学生・卒業生（1986-2003 年 短期大学部英米語科を含む）および英語英文学科の教員、名誉会員、特別会員で構成され、英語・英文学の研究と会員相互の親睦を主な目的とし、会員の会費により運営されている。2017 年に設立 50 周年記念事業を展開した。本書のもととなった English Playbook（2018）もその事業の一環である。

同志社女子大学英語英文学会
〒602-0893 京都市上京区今出川通寺町西入玄武町 602-1
TEL & FAX: 075-251-4193
E-mail: egakkai@dwc.doshisha.ac.jp
URL: https://www.egakkaidwcla.com

English Playbook

2024 年 4 月 1 日　発行

発　行　　同志社女子大学英語英文学会
　　　　　The English Society of Doshisha Women's College of Liberal Arts
　　　　　〒602-0893　京都市上京区今出川通寺町西入玄武町 602-1
　　　　　TEL&FAX　075-251-4193
　　　　　E-mail　　　egakkai@dwc.doshisha.ac.jp
　　　　　URL　　　　https://www.egakkaidwcla.com

発行所　　英宝社

印刷所　　日本ハイコム株式会社